Please remember that this is a library book,
and that it belongs only temporarily to each
person who uses it. Be considerate. Do
not write in this, or any, library book.

The WIRED TOWER:
Perspectives on the Impact of the Internet on Higher Education

WITHDRAWN

ISBN 0-13-042829-9

90000

9 780130 428295

FINANCIAL TIMES

Prentice Hall

In an increasingly competitive world, it is quality of thinking that gives an edge—an idea that opens new doors, a technique that solves a problem, or an insight that simply helps make sense of it all.

We work with leading authors in the various arenas of business and finance to bring cutting-edge thinking and best learning practice to a global market.

It is our goal to create world-class print publications and electronic products that give readers knowledge and understanding which can then be applied, whether studying or at work.

To find out more about our business products, you can visit us at www.ft-ph.com.

Pearson
Education

THE WIRED TOWER:

PERSPECTIVES ON

THE IMPACT OF THE INTERNET

ON HIGHER EDUCATION

MATTHEW SERBIN PITTINSKY

An Imprint of PEARSON EDUCATION

Upper Saddle River, NJ • New York • London • San Francisco • Toronto • Sydney
Tokyo • Singapore • Hong Kong • Cape Town • Madrid
Paris • Milan • Munich • Amsterdam

www.ft-ph.com

Library of Congress Cataloging-in-Publication Data

A catalog record for this book can be obtained from the Library of Congress.

378.173
P68w
2003

Editorial/Production Supervision: Nick Radhuber
Acquisitions Editor: Tim Moore
Marketing Manager: Bryan Gambrel
Manufacturing Manager: Maura Zaldivar
Cover Design Director: Jerry Votta
Cover Design: Anthony Gemmellaro
Interior Design: Gail Cocker-Bogusz

© 2003 Pearson Education, Inc.
Publishing as Prentice Hall PTR
Upper Saddle River, NJ 07458

Prentice Hall books are widely used by corporations and government agencies for training, marketing, and resale.

The publisher offers discounts on this book when ordered in bulk quantities.
For more information, contact: Corporate Sales Department, Phone: 800-382-3419;
Fax: 201-236-7141; E-mail: corpsales@prenhall.com; or write: Prentice Hall PTR,
Corp. Sales Dept., One Lake Street, Upper Saddle River, NJ 07458.

Printed in the United States of America

10 9 8 7 6 5 4 3 2 1

ISBN 0-13-042829-9

Pearson Education LTD.
Pearson Education Australia PTY, Limited
Pearson Education Singapore, Pte. Ltd.
Pearson Education North Asia Ltd.
Pearson Education Canada, Ltd.
Pearson Educación de Mexico, S.A. de C.V.
Pearson Education—Japan
Pearson Education Malaysia, Pte. Ltd.

FINANCIAL TIMES PRENTICE HALL BOOKS

For more information, please go to www.ft-ph.com

Tom Osenton
Customer Share Marketing: How the World's Great Marketers Unlock Profits from Customer Loyalty

Richard W. Paul and Linda Elder
Critical Thinking: Tools for Taking Charge of Your Professional and Personal Life

Matthew Serbin Pittinsky, Editor
The Wired Tower: Perspectives on the Impact of the Internet on Higher Education

W. Alan Randolph and Barry Z. Posner
Checkered Flag Projects: 10 Rules for Creating and Managing Projects that Win, Second Edition

Stephen P. Robbins
The Truth About Managing People...And Nothing but the Truth

Fernando Robles, Françoise Simon, and Jerry Haar
Winning Strategies for the New Latin Markets

Jeff Saperstein and Daniel Rouach
Creating Regional Wealth in the Innovation Economy: Models, Perspectives, and Best Practices

Eric G. Stephan and Wayne R. Pace
Powerful Leadership: How to Unleash the Potential in Others and Simplify Your Own Life

Jonathan Wight
Saving Adam Smith: A Tale of Wealth, Transformation, and Virtue

Yoram J. Wind and Vijay Mahajan, with Robert Gunther
Convergence Marketing: Strategies for Reaching the New Hybrid Consumer

CONTENTS

PREFACE

In April 2001, 350 educational leaders and academics gathered in Washington, DC to discuss the Internet's impact on higher education. As a summit of sorts, speakers from academe, business, and government grappled with the fundamental nature of e-learning—the adoption of and reliance on the Internet for teaching and learning. Organized around a theme of transformation versus evolution, speakers such as Columbia University Teacher's College President Arthur Levine, VerticalNet Chairman Mark Walsh, researcher and technology luminary Carol

Twigg, author and New York University professor Neil Postman, and others presented compelling perspectives on the topic.

This book draws on the talks given at the meeting, tackling this question: Is the impact of e-learning on higher education transformative or simply evolutionary? The genesis of *The Wired Tower*—the post e-learning Ivory Tower—lay in the desire to package the wonderfully diverse, yet interrelated perspectives that the various authors shared in their presentations. At a time of change, it attempts to elevate the microquestions of e-learning often tackled in classroom-based anecdotes, to a macrolevel of industry history, structure, and change. The topics are mostly distinct—from international issues to Wall Street—yet the arguments made are all critical to shaping a view of the Internet's impact on academe.

Through my work as chairman of Blackboard Inc., I have long argued that the promise of the Internet is one that will likely sustain the traditional campus model, rather than transform it into something foreign or new. To be sure, over time small ideas, such as the delivery of courses to alumni online, may turn into big ideas such as a "warranty" on knowledge where tuition provides not only the initial period of degree study, but also an ongoing return—via the Web—to the campus for additional coursework throughout life. Indeed, if the dot-com world is truly a guide, near-term evolutionary changes, developed over time, will lead to a

fundamentally transformed way of delivering and supporting the instructional process in higher education.

As you move from chapter to chapter, the contributors
to this book demonstrate firsthand that a compelling argument can be made on both sides of the debate. Despite its
image as an enterprise slow to change, if you look back in
history, higher education has indeed experienced periods of
great change and flux, albeit few and far between. Over
time, more facilities, more research, more specialization,
more students, more remedial courses, bigger budgets, and
different recruitment strategies have all changed the face of
higher education; small changes at first, but dramatic ones
by the end.

Looking back at the 350 years since Harvard's founding,
at least three momentous developments stand out: passage
of the GI Bill, which brought unprecedented access to higher education; establishment of land-grant colleges, which
provided a vast new network of research and development
institutions that helped transform the American economy
in the post-Civil War era; and the founding of Johns Hopkins
University, which was to serve as a model for large science-
oriented institutions. Most recently, the creation and explosion of community colleges in the post-World War II period,
and the growth of affirmative action policies with the passage of the Higher Education Act of 1965, have also fostered
dramatic change.

THE PERSPECTIVES IN CONTEXT

To help structure the compilation, I open the book with a short chapter developed to frame the debate and introduce several of the key themes that emerge throughout. Starting with a discussion of the many prognostications made of late about the dire impact that e-learning will have on higher education, Chapter 1, "Transformation Through Evolution," reflects on the track record of similar predictions in the e-commerce world and identifies four key drivers for e-learning that are core to the future of higher education.

In Chapter 2, "Higher Education: A Revolution Externally, Evolution Internally," Columbia University Teacher's College President Arthur Levine identifies key forces shaping the higher education landscape today and applies them to the historic mission of universities. Levine provides a compelling blueprint of what needs to be preserved and what will surely be changed, as technology increasingly has a transformative and invigorating impact on higher learning.

Next, in Chapter 3, "The Business of Education," Wall Street equity analyst Greg Cappelli paints a comprehensive picture of the current state of higher education and the key e-learning trends within. He illustrates the size of the postsecondary market in the U.S., the composition of institutional spending on technology, the growth of Internet usage and access by faculty and students, the nature of that use, and the economic and demographic pressures behind launching e-learning initiatives.

Building on Cappelli's U.S. industry backdrop, in Chapter 4, "The Emerging Global e-Learning Industry," Georgetown University professor Martin Irvine tackles post-secondary e-learning from an international perspective. He mixes a review of overall statistics and common adoption drivers with a region-by-region consideration of leading projects and unique challenges and opportunities.

Whereas Chapters 1 through 4 are intended to form a basic foundation for thinking about the scale of the higher education industry in the U.S. and abroad, and major e-learning trends at a macro level, in Chapter 5, "Quality, Cost, and Access: The Case for Redesign," Carol Twigg takes us down to the nitty-gritty specifics of implementation and design. By drawing on her work at the Center for Academic Transformation, Twigg provides a framework for how technology can be harnessed through successful course redesign to improve quality and lower costs. Her generous use of examples from campuses engaged in a variety of redesign projects illustrates specific projects where Levine's trends are well at work today.

Continuing our movement from trends to implementation, Donald Spicer uses Chapter 6, "Where the Rubber Meets the Road: An On-Campus Perspective of a CIO," to place us in the shoes of a typical university chief information officer (CIO). Tasked with the responsibility of supporting innovations in administration and pedagogy, the roles of the CIO and campus technology organizations in general are changing dramatically. Nowhere is this more true than at the University of Maryland system, where traditional residential programs, adult education programs, and online for-profit programs are among the nation's most successful and innovative. In his chapter, Spicer outlines the technology challenges in supporting these programs from a cost, policy, and staffing perspective.

To address the potential downside of technology's increasing impact on education, the last outside contribution to the book is a chapter by professor and social critic Neil Postman in which he demonstrates a healthy skepticism. In Chapter 7, "Questioning Media," Postman presents five key questions that must be asked before adopting new technologies—questions that critique technology adoption in both academic and popular society. The result is a wise and often witty consideration of the reality underlining the perceived benefits of information technology.

Finally, in Chapter 8, "Five Great Promises of e-learning," I close with a second minichapter that rounds out Chapter 1 with a crystal-ball discussion of five key transformative e-learning trends that may emerge over the near future.

NOTE ABOUT LANGUAGE

As Postman describes in Chapter 7 of this book, all new media have influences above and beyond their original purpose. Already, due in large part to the influence of the business side of e-learning, a change in vocabulary is underfoot in which "courses" have become "content," "universities" are "content providers," alma maters describe themselves as "brands," the learning process is characterized as "Web traffic" and "page views," and perhaps most distressing of all, "students" are described as "users." As an editor, I can assure you that the perspectives shared in the book, on both sides of the debate, begin from a love for and deep respect of the unique and special characteristics of academe. As such, the vocabulary of the discussion avoids e-jargon in favor of traditional education terminology.

ACKNOWLEDGMENTS

By definition, the editor of a compiled work owes the success of his project to the support and contribution of others. First and foremost, I owe a debt of gratitude to the authors whose chapters provide the core arguments weaved together in this volume for the first time to address the topic of postsecondary e-learning. The strength of each chapter speaks for itself; of course, any shortcomings are mine alone as I endeavored to pare them down and integrate them into the book as a whole.

As mentioned in the introduction, this book is the result of the ideas put forward at the 2001 Blackboard Summit. I would like to thank Courtney Caro, Nicole Hyde, and Michael Stanton for their hard work in shaping the program that ultimately brought these chapter contributors together. In addition, I would like to thank Michael Chasen, Blackboard's CEO and co-founder, and my friend, for his constant support of me and this project.

As a first-time editor and author, I am truly fortunate to have been aided by two great teams—one working directly with me and the other at Prentice Hall Financial Times. Assisting me in the management of the project, and tackling more than their fair share of editing, was the dynamic team of Bob Hochstein and Shelly O'Horo. Both have dedicated countless hours to the book and their contributions can be seen on every page. I owe them my sincerest thanks and appreciation. Similarly, Tim Moore and Russ Hall at Prentice Hall Financial Times were generous in their support and nurturing of a first timer.

Finally, I would like to thank my family who remind me every day that they put me on this earth, took good care of me, and therefore deserve a healthy amount of credit for everything I do. They are right. My passion for education is the direct result of my parents, Janet, a truly gifted teacher, and Bernard, an outstanding university administrator and school board president. They, in addition to the entire clan—Larry, Jill, Scott, Todd, Harris, and Marc—have been wonderfully supportive.

Newest to the family is my wife, Julie Renee Cohen, and her family, Jesse, Joni, and Elana. Julie is the love of my life, my best friend, and someone whose work every day on behalf of young children sets the bar high for me indeed. For her support and encouragement go my last and deepest thanks!

—*Matthew Pittinsky*
WASHINGTON, DC

1

TRANSFORMATION
THROUGH
EVOLUTION

The *New York Times Magazine* highlighted an article on its cover entitled "Online U—How Entrepreneurs and Academic Radicals Are Breaking Down the Walls of the University." The thrust of the story led one to believe that the Internet could cause the undermining, if not ultimately the elimination, of some of the nation's traditional colleges and universities, replaced by virtual universities in cyberspace.

Just a few months later, in the February 2000 issue of *Mother Jones* magazine, a featured article claimed the screaming headline, "A Campus of One . . . Who Needs Professors When the Online University Is Only a Click Away?"

Most recently, in a speech made during the summer of 2000, Michael Moe, a former Merrill Lynch analyst, warned, "The Internet is all about disproportionate gain to leaders. Eventually, it's going to turn the higher education market on its head. The 100 or so leading universities will do great; the other 3,400 are going to have to figure out how to make themselves relevant to the new economy."

These are clearly heady times for academic administrators, faculty, students, parents, investors, and any citizen who believes that our system of higher education is a cornerstone of America's economy and society. Almost daily, predictions like the ones just cited warn of dire changes; the logical consequences of the Internet and information technology will, they warn, play out dramatically across the college and university landscape.

FROM DOT-COM TO DOT-EDU

If the opening quotes sound familiar, it is because many of the same arguments were made about the impact of the Internet on the business world. With the collapse of the "dot-com bubble" in April 2000, we have seen a reversal in thinking; unrestrained euphoria has melted into unquestioned skepticism. Much ballyhooed Internet companies have become history, rather than vehicles for changing history. Much maligned traditional businesses have once again proved their staying power. The lesson that business is business is being discovered anew by a youthful generation of would-be entrepreneurs. Brick-and-mortar factories and companies, as well as "brick-and-click" companies—traditional businesses that use the Internet to become more efficient—have triumphed over brash "click-and-click" startups that were purportedly going to transform the corporate landscape.

Proving the adage of deja vu all over again, similar trends are already forming in higher education. In July 2001, Temple University quietly shut down the Virtual Temple for-profit spin-off it had created in late 1999. Four months later in November 2001, New York University announced the closing of its for-profit distance-learning venture *NYU Online*. Even the University of Maryland's successful *UMUC Online* has faced regulatory difficulties, as is discussed in a later chapter of the book.

Yet for every article in the *Chronicle of Higher Education* announcing the end of a postsecondary Internet venture, two more can be found describing an e-learning project that was successful, although with perhaps more modest aspirations. At institutions as diverse as the University of Texas Telecampus, University of Phoenix Online, Penn State World Campus, and Dallas Community College District alone, more than 100,000 enrollments are learning online. In the fall of 2001, nearly 30 percent of all campus-based college enrollments arrived to find the Web a meaningful part of their course administration and delivery.

DeSalles University is developing an online MBA program for deaf students and the hearing impaired. It will begin operating in Fall 2002 and the language used will be text-based supported by graphics. Having grown up with sign language, many of the enrollments will simply be thought of as students with a different first language. At Skidmore College, a course on Harlem's culture highlighting contributions and clashes is given both in class and online. Online students read summaries of lectures and discussion at their own convenience—a hybrid model.

Beyond sparking dramatic new models, the Internet is most commonly (and successfully) enriching and reinforcing "traditional" higher education in a variety of ways. For example, through campus Web portals, students can register for courses, make appointments to meet with advisors, check the syllabus for courses, reach everyone on campus through electronic bulletin boards and email, and check grades and exam schedules. Collaboration between faculty and students, which is so critical to the instructional process, is being made easier with Web discussion boards. Cooperation among faculty is being simplified as documents are shared online. In short, rather than falling into irrelevance due to the Internet, campus life is simply becoming more integrated and more connected—thanks specifically to Internet technologies. This is only the beginning.

THE ROOTS OF E-LEARNING

In many ways, the success of more incremental approaches to the deployment of Internet technologies on campus should come as no surprise. A careful examination of the roots of the current boom in e-learning reveals that its growth lies in several long developing trends of American higher education, some of which have nothing to do with the Internet per se, and all of which were being addressed long before e-learning. It is *these* trends that are the true drivers of change and successful e-learning programs are those that are most connected to them. Indeed, four are identified and reinforced through the book, as follows.

1. *The renewed focus on pedagogy and the learner.* With the explosive growth of higher education enrollments over the past few decades, a growing chorus of critics and reformers have argued for an increased focus on the quality of instruction. Although we are all familiar with the age-old debate about the primacy of research versus teaching in an institution's mission, the issue of quality instruction involves much more. Issues of faculty training, course evaluation, analysis of learning outcomes, and increased focus on the learner and learning styles are all part and parcel of an increased consciousness of the need to think

about how instruction is delivered in higher education. Against this backdrop, it is no surprise that on many campuses, the primary support organizations for e-learning are the centers that were originally developed to focus on improving faculty teaching skills in general. The adoption of virtual learning environments has been largely driven by faculty who see the Internet as a solution to an instructional problem, not "technothusiasts" who simply enjoy the technology. Although some worry that the demands of e-learning are monopolizing the resources of instructional support teams, in reality it works both ways. Indeed, the very act of creating a course Web site is one that demonstrates thoughtfulness on the part of the faculty member as to how he or she is going to teach the course; this thoughtfulness typically leads to other nontechnology changes in a course's design.

2. *The movement of technology from the back office to the front office.* Although higher education can rightfully lay claim to a number of critical information technology breakthroughs, including the Internet, conventional wisdom argues that it generally lags the private sector in the implementation of these technologies. For example, colleges and universities took much longer than their corporate counterparts to adopt integrated commer-

cial systems for managing back office operations such as student records, finance, and human resources. This trend remained true as corporations transformed their corporate Web sites from brochures to vehicles for doing business. Only recently have universities begun to accept applications, donations, course registrations, and the like over the Web. Most recently, corporate America has recognized the need for technology to transform the front office—those services that face the consumer of the business—investing in systems that improve activities such as support, service, customer relationships, and the like. Only recently has higher education begun to think of its student-centric units in quite the same way, and e-learning is a core component of this trend. Today's student expects a technology-supported experience from application to registration to donation. Campuses are scrambling to deploy campus Web portals that offer everything from health center scheduling to registration for season tickets to football games. Because the core daily activity of a student is teaching and learning, creating a baseline Web environment for instruction has become the core of a broader front office expansion of technology.

3. *The high-stakes search for new funding sources.* Certainly a significant context for the growth of e-learning is money—more specifically, the need to tap new financial sources. For some institutions, financial opportunity has been the primary public rationale given for the creation of for-profit subsidiaries that have initial public offering (IPO) potential. For others, it is less stated but no less important. At a time when state funding is decreasing, tuition rates have begun to max out, and the cost of doing business only increases, colleges and universities have become increasingly entrepreneurial in their sources of new revenue streams. The growth of extension programs, executive education programs, certificate programs, travel programs, and other branches of the traditional curriculum all serve to educate broader audiences, but with the added benefit of doing so with much higher profit margins than traditional undergraduate education provides.

4. *The pressure and opportunity to serve new enrollments and markets.* Perhaps the most frequently mentioned context for the sudden rise in postsecondary e-learning is the transition of America into a knowledge economy. More than ever, human capital is the key asset of corpora-

tions and the primary determinate of our career potential and livelihood. More people are seeking advanced education more frequently in their lives than ever before. As a result, states such as Utah estimate a doubling of their public institution enrollments over the next 10 years. The strain is particularly acute in areas such as education, nursing, information technology, and other professional disciplines that face workforce shortages. One implication is the rise of the for-profit segment of higher education that offers a focused, cost-effective degree "product" for the market. Higher education has experience working with corporate America as an originator of research and development, but the demands of playing a similar role as the ongoing developer of professional capacity are new and touch the core activity of the campus. As a result, it is quite political and the uncertainty facing university decision makers cannot be overstated. However, in this uncertainty, and with the revenue potential mentioned earlier in mind, the new markets placing demands on higher education offer fertile ground for the development of e-learning programs that can deliver courses to broader audiences, free of the limitations of geography and time.

THE POTENTIAL FOR GREAT CHANGE

Understanding the roots of e-learning, the question of transformation versus evolution that serves to organize this book may not be as binary as it seems. Few should expect (or desire) the face-to-face experience of undergraduate and graduate education to go the way of the 8-track tape player. The question now is not whether virtual universities and other Internet-driven structural changes in higher education will take root and mature. Instead, the question is whether it will happen suddenly through high-profile initiatives that create change all at once, or whether the quiet revolution occurring in more traditional classrooms will, over time, get us to the same point, building on existing conventions.

The Internet offers many obvious and powerful opportunities to reinforce the traditional higher education campus model. As an example, distance learning initiatives have much to learn from the simplicity of peer-to-peer communication among students inside and outside a traditional classroom. Traditional courses can certainly benefit from the rich online collaborative environments that have been well implemented in online distance learning programs. What is transformative is the experience of the course—learning throughout a semester constantly connected to a course community that is one click away. What is evolutionary is the pedagogy—the belief that peer-to-peer communication is a core process for effective education.

As is well discussed in the next five chapters of the book, e-learning has risen to the top of the higher education agenda because of its potential to open new revenue sources, improve instructional approaches, expand the support of technology outside of the back office, and serve new markets at a time of great demand. If the potential is turned into reality, e-learning will be transformative. However, the path toward success is one that will likely be made through incremental changes that evolve over time. Although the experience of education will surely be different, the technology inevitably will be driven by pedagogy, ensuring that our core values remain the same.

2

HIGHER EDUCATION: A REVOLUTION EXTERNALLY, EVOLUTION INTERNALLY

—Arthur Levine
PRESIDENT OF TEACHER'S COLLEGE, COLUMBIA UNIVERSITY

Dig deep into the arguments that define the debate about transformation and evolution in e-learning, and it is clear that there are broader influences at work than simply the use of the Internet for teaching and learning. Even prior to the trends being wrought by e-learning, the industry of higher education was poised for dramatic growth and change. As we shift from an industrial economy to a knowledge economy—a time when what people know is their greatest financial asset and that of their employer—our

13

nation's largest knowledge industry—academe—was bound to be impacted.

Consider just a few of the ways in which the landscape is changing: There are for-profit companies competing against nonprofits for student populations. There are enrollment booms across the nation overloading our capacity to serve them. There are new types of learners—older and more professionally oriented—who are coming back to the institution more often and with different expectations. There are cost pressures and new types of funding sources, such as corporate sponsorships, that carry different strings. There are subtle changes occurring in the nature of faculty; for example, the greater use of adjuncts and professional instructors. All of these nips and tucks in our system of higher education have altered the face of university life as much, if not more than, e-learning alone. When combined with the explosive adoption of Internet technologies, the full force of what is happening takes form. Indeed, it is the convergence of industry and technology change that is the most potent.

As Columbia University Teacher's College President Arthur Levine notes in Chapter 2, education as an industry can be compared to health care just a few years ago—bureaucratic, dominated by nonprofits, heavily influenced by government, considered a fundamental right by consumers, immune to pricing pressures, and for all of these reasons rife for dramatic restructuring. Levine's *essay opens the book with an industry look at how higher education is changing, by situating e-learning as an important, but not sole, contributor to the change. For the uninitiated, his chapter paints a straightforward and compelling picture of the state of higher education. For those of us who live these changes everyday, he succinctly describes the logical consequences of today's trends on tomorrow's campus.*

Arthur Levine is President and Professor of Education at Teacher's College, Columbia University. He received his bachelor's degree from Brandeis University and his PhD from the State University of New York at Buffalo. Prior to his appointment at Teacher's College, he served as Chair of the Higher Education program and Chair of the Institute for Educational Management at the Harvard Graduate School of Education. Levine is the author of dozens of articles and reviews. His most recent book is When Hope and Fear Collide: A Portrait of Today's College Student *(Levine, A., and Cureton, J., San Francisco, Jossey-Bass, 1998). Among other volumes are* Beating the Odds: How the Poor Get to College *(Levine, A., and Nidiffer, J., San Francisco, Jossey-Bass, 1995),* Higher Learning in America *(Levine, A., and Nidiffer, J., San Francisco, Jossey-Bass, 1985),* Shaping Higher Education's Future: Demographic Realities and Opportunities: 1990-2000 *(Levine A. and Associates, San Francisco, Jossey-Bass, 1989),* When Dreams and Heroes Died: A Portrait of

Today's College Student *(Levine, A., San Francisco, Jossey-Bass, 1980)*, Handbook on Undergraduate Curriculum *(Levine, A., and Green, J., San Francisco, Jossey-Bass, 1985)*, Quest for Common Learning *(Levine, A., and Nidiffer, San Francisco, Jossey-Bass, 1995)*, Opportunity in Adversity *(Levine, A., and Green, J., San Francisco, Jossey-Bass, 1995), and* Why Innovation Fails *(Albany, State University of New York Press, 1980). A 1982 Guggenheim Fellowship winner, Levine's other awards include a 1998 listing in* Change *magazine as "One of the most Outstanding Leaders in the Academic Community;" the 1996 Council of Independent College's Academic Leadership Award; the Educational Press Association's Annual Award for Writing in 1981, 1989, and 1993; and 15 honorary degrees. He has served as consultant to more than 250 colleges and named 1999–2001 Carnegie Fellow, formerly Senior Fellow at the Carnegie Foundation and Carnegie Council for Policy Studies in Higher Education (1975–1982).*

The organizing question of this book—whether the Internet's impact on higher education will be transformative or evolutionary—is a timely one. To address this question up front and succinctly, I believe that higher education is on the eve of a revolution and that five forces will drive it.

First, our economy has shifted from an industrial to an information base. This means the population will require more education to function in the new economy and education must continue throughout life as the "half-life" of knowledge gets shorter and shorter.

Second, the demographics of higher education have changed. The new majority of college students are older, part-time, and working. Higher education is not the most pressing concern in their lives. It is often overshadowed by jobs, spouses or partners, families, and friends. These students want higher education that is convenient, is efficient in providing service, offers quality instruction, and is low in price. They are prime candidates for stripped-down versions of college without electives and student services. They are excellent prospects for distance learning, available in their homes or offices.

There is also a growing population of traditional-age college students with numbers booming particularly in the West and the South. California, for example, is facing a boom of a half-million new students. This raises larger questions about how the states should respond to an inadequate number of physical campuses—build more or create e-learning programs.

There is also an anticipated dramatic expansion in international student numbers as English becomes the world language and U.S. higher education remains the global postsecondary leader.

Third, new technologies are likely to have a profound influence on higher education. They are the largest megaphone in postsecondary history allowing colleges and universities to reach larger numbers than ever before in history, at any time and any place.

Fourth, the private sector is investing in higher education at a greater rate than ever before. Viewing postsecondary education as the next health care industry—low in productivity, high in cost, poor in management, and uninvolved in technology—profit seekers believe collegiate education is in need of a private-sector makeover. Indeed the largest private university in the United States today, the University of Phoenix, is regionally accredited and traded on the NASDAQ.

Fifth and finally, there is a growing convergence between knowledge-producing organizations—publishers, television, libraries, museums, concert halls, and universities. All are using new technologies to distribute their content to reach larger and larger audiences. The result is that all are producing things that look increasingly like courses. The publisher Harcourt has created a university and PBS is now the largest educator of science teachers in the country.

THE COMING REVOLUTION

I believe the results of these changes are likely to be dramatic. A number of the changes are, in fact, already well underway.

Higher education providers will become even more numerous and more diverse. The survival of some institutions, especially less selective private colleges with small endowments and large programs in adult education, will be increasingly threatened by both domestic and foreign for-profit institutions, as well as nonprofit competitors like libraries and museums that also have entered the educational marketplace. Moreover, technological capabilities are encouraging the rise of global universities, which transcend national boundaries. The most successful institutions will be those that can respond the quickest and offer a high-quality education to an international student body.

As a result, we should expect new brand names and a new hierarchy of quality in higher education institutions. Why should a credential from Microsoft University or the British Open University be less prestigious than one from a regional state college? The answer to this question will have a fundamental influence on everything from standards to quality control mechanisms such as accreditation.

Three basic types of colleges and universities are emerging. They are *brick universities,* or traditional residential institutions; *click universities,* or new, usually commercial virtual universities, like Unext.com and Jones International University; and *brick-and-click* universities, a combination of the first two. If current research on e-commerce is correct, the most competitive and attractive higher education institutions will be brick-and-click universities. Consumers appreciate the convenience, ease, and freedom of services online, but they also want a physical space where they can interact with others and obtain expert advice and assistance face-to-face.

Although it may prove clear that the brick-and-click model is the best, it is less clear which type of institution will get there first. Either the for-profit sector will buy bricks before traditional colleges develop the capacity to operate in the click environment, or just the opposite may occur.

Higher education is becoming more individualized; students, not institutions, will set the educational agenda. Increasingly, students will come from diverse backgrounds and will have a widening variety of educational needs. New technologies will enable them to receive their education at any time and any place—on a campus, in the office, at home, in the car, or on vacation. Each student will be able to choose from a multitude of knowledge providers the form of instruction and courses most consistent with how he or she learns.

The impact on colleges when providing services for students with such heterogeneous backgrounds and individualized educational goals is significant. Institutions long have prided themselves on their ability to create a strong sense of identity and community. Online education complicates this issue even more; brick-and-mortar campuses can no longer rely solely on proximity to build community.

The focus of higher education is shifting from teaching to learning. Colleges currently emphasize a commonality of process based on *seat time,* or the amount of time each student is taught. Students study for a defined number of hours, earn credits for each hour of study, and, after earning a specified number of credits, earn a degree. With the increasing number of educational providers, the individualization of education, and the growing diversity of the student body, however, that commonality of process is likely to be lost. The focus will shift to the outcomes that students achieve. Time will become the variable and learning the constant.

Such a development raises very large questions about the meaning of a two-year or four-year degree. It also shifts the definition of excellence from the institution's selectivity in admitting students to the value that the institution demonstrably adds to each student's learning experience.

We also should expect other new forces to gain momentum.

Faculty members will become increasingly independent of colleges and universities. The most renowned faculty members, those able to attract tens of thousands of students in an international marketplace, will become like rock stars. It is only a matter of time before we see the equivalent of an academic William Morris Agency. With a worldwide market in the hundreds of millions of students, a talent agent will be able to bring to a professor a book deal with Random House, a weekly program on PBS, a consulting contract with IBM, commercial endorsement opportunities, and a distance-learning course with a for-profit company in a total package worth $5 million.

The names of world-class professors will probably be far more important than the institution for which they work. Such a development will be analogous to the changes experienced in Hollywood when the dominance of the studios gave way to the star power of the actors themselves.

Institutions of higher education must ask how they can create communities that are sufficiently vital to attract and retain faculty members in such an environment. There is a very real risk of the rich getting richer and the poor getting poorer, with only a handful of very prestigious, well-endowed institutions able to afford the most distinguished professors. Indeed, the current faculty–institution relationship has evolved over hundreds of years and influences many aspects of a campus. For example, greater power by faculty will surely mean changes in institutional governance. The future of tenure may well be questioned if the most sought-after professors leave the academy or become itinerant.

Degrees will wither in importance. Today, the meaning of a degree varies in content and quality, depending on the college. In essence, we offer thousands of different degrees, even if they are called by the same name. A degree now signifies a period of successful college attendance, the class rank indicates the relative success of the student, and the name of the college marks the quality of the degree.

However, with the change in emphasis from institutional process to educational outcomes, degrees will become far less meaningful. A transcript of each student's competencies, including the specific information that the student knows or the skills that he or she can perform, will be far more desirable.

Colleges now have a virtual monopoly on higher education credentials. If degrees become less important in a world offering limitless educational choices, the traditional drivers of enrollment may be up for grabs. Why would a student stay at the same college for periods of up to five years if degrees give way to specific competencies? Residential institutions may be the hardest hit as the nature of degrees change. Traditional collegiate life may become the province of only the most affluent in our society who have the leisure and money to afford it.

Every person will have an educational passport. In the future, each person's education will occur not only in a cornucopia of different settings and geographic locales, but also via a plethora of different educational providers. As traditional degrees lose importance, the nation will need to establish a central bureau that records each person's educational achievements—however and wherever they were gained—and that provides documentation. Such an educational passport, or portfolio, will record a student's lifetime educational history.

We will need common standards for naming and assessing those achievements. Our decentralized system of higher education makes such a bureau difficult to accomplish. Indeed, it is not even obvious which agency should take the lead: government accrediting agencies or the private sector.

Dollars will follow the students more than the educators. With the growth in educational providers and the emphasis on outcomes, public and private financial supporters will increasingly invest in the educational consumer rather than the expanding grab bag of organizations that offer collegiate instruction. It's quite possible that federal and state aid that currently supports institutions of higher education will be transferred directly to students.

Such a trend will add to the enormous questions about how to ensure standards of quality among the increasing number of new providers. It will also require us to ask how academic freedom, which demands institutional autonomy, can be preserved when colleges are forced to be as market-driven and consumer-oriented as most commercial organizations are today. How can institutions remain economically viable when financial support shifts more to consumers, faculty members grow more independent, and degrees fade in importance?

What I have described in the past paragraphs is, in some sense, a ghost of Christmas future. Although the trends are no more than one individual's halting attempt to predict things to come, I have no doubt that the forces buffeting higher education today are powerful and will change it considerably. My fear is that America's colleges will ignore them and the important questions that they demand we confront—or that, simply through complacency or the glacial speed of our decision-making processes, we will fail to respond in time to help shape tomorrow.

In the early years of the Industrial Revolution, the Yale Report of 1828 asked whether the needs of a changing society required either major or minor changes in higher education. The report concluded that it had asked the wrong question. The right question was this: What is the purpose of higher education?

All of the questions that I've raised have their deepest roots in that fundamental question. Once more faced with a society in motion, we must not only ask that question again, but must actively pursue answers if our colleges and universities are to retain their vitality in a dramatically different world.

THE COMING EVOLUTION

Understanding the fundamental mission of our nation's diverse colleges and universities is the key to mapping where in this continuum between brick-and-click institutions will land. Surely we do not want all U.S. higher education institutions to morph into click or brick-and-click entities. There is no need for 3,600 institutions to provide online courses. I expect there will be a small number of online educators that dominate the marketplace. Many people are going to want a traditional campus experience, including students, and the parents who have waited 18 years for them to leave home, among others. My greatest fear is that in years to come this experience will be available to only the most affluent, best, and brightest in the nation. Others will be forced into cheaper click education.

In any case, traditional colleges face two very real dangers. The first is that they will ignore or move glacially as higher education decision making is prone to do, into the digital era. The result would be an anachronistic and infirm set of institutions, having been left far behind during the revolution. The second danger is that traditional higher education will rush into, or worse yet, will be pushed headlong into the new digital economy and abandon what is sacred about higher education, those things that no other social institution is capable of providing. This would rob higher education of its very reason for being.

Let's consider what is sacred. Universities engage in three activities: discovery and creation of new knowledge, preservation and dissemination of knowledge, and application of knowledge to solving social problems. It engages in these functions in a way no other social organization does.

THE DISCOVERY AND CREATION
OF NEW KNOWLEDGE

There are many, many organizations in our society that engage in research, but the university is the only one that is committed to the open and unfettered search for truth. The university is intended to be a place in which any question can be asked and any answer can be found. This ideal has never been achieved, but there is no organization that has more closely approached it or held the commitment to do so more central.

To make this search possible, society has permitted the university to ground itself in academic freedom, a set of rights that does not exist in any other social institution. Academic freedom derives from the term *lehrfreiheit,* a practice imported from the 19th century German university, which has come to mean the freedom of a professor to carry out research and teach the results of that research in and out of the classroom, and on and off campus without social and institutional interference.

The academic community experienced five decades of well-publicized intrusions from the 1870s to World War I by

the church, government, boards of trustees, business interests, and influential donors. At universities all across the
country from Stanford to Yale and Vanderbilt to Wisconsin,
professors were fired or threatened with discharge for taking what were judged to be the wrong sides of controversial
issues such as Darwinism, public ownership of railroads,
immigration, alcohol prohibition, bimetalism, and U.S.
entry into World War I. The academic remedy for these intrusions was the creation of tenure, a mechanism designed
to ensure professors' academic freedom by granting them
permanent appointments or lifelong employment after a
probationary period.

This system of academic freedom and tenure has frequently been criticized for its weaknesses. Unchecked by
disciplined peer review, academic freedom can become academic license. Much too often academic freedom is con-
fused with unconditional or absolute professorial
autonomy, the ability of a faculty member to do whatever
he or she wishes—deciding whether to turn in grades in a
timely fashion, whether to hold office hours, or even
whether to convene classes. Tenure can also become a vehicle for sheltering unproductive or poorly performing professors from being dismissed.

Even with these limitations, academic freedom is essential to higher education and tenure is the best vehicle we
know for ensuring that it continues. It is hard to argue that
improvements cannot or should not be made, particularly

in light of the end of the mandatory retirement laws, which means that a professor can remain on the job far longer today than the average of 30 years when tenure rules were promulgated.

However, it is a fragile system that must not be undermined by comparisons with business, which is not in the market of discovering new knowledge for knowledge's sake, or of offering its employees lifetime engagements. The elements that encourage security and risk taking in the for-profit sector, such as equity in the business and golden parachutes, are absent in the university.

PRESERVATION AND TRANSMISSION OF ETERNAL TRUTHS

Higher education disseminates the truths it discovers. Today, we tend to call our truths *knowledge*—the ideas, concepts, theories, understandings, and even questions that need to be preserved. The university is at once a repository of knowledge, old and new, and the transmitter of that knowledge. The nation's shift from an industrial to an information economy has given the repository function greater social importance than ever before in history. That's because in today's economy, the new sources of wealth come from knowledge and communication rather than the natural resources and physical labor that characterize industrial societies.

In the past our society was national in focus and put a premium on physical capital—plant and machinery. In contrast, our information society is global with an emphasis on intellectual capital—knowledge and the people who produce it. Intellectual capital is the gold of the Information Age and no organization has a greater accumulation of intellectual content or knowledge, and intellectual capital or faculty with the capacity to create, apply, and disseminate new and existing knowledge than the university. In short, the university has the potential to be the primary economic engine of modern society.

But it is more than this, too. The university's role as a repository for knowledge long ago made it into something akin to a truth teller for society. We expect the university to serve as a neutral social critic, continually evaluating and assessing the society against all we know about the past and present. This is a requirement for maintaining a democratic society. A healthy university is essential for countering those who would dismiss history, deny the laws of science, or dismantle democratic institutions. Though frail in the face of powerful antidemocratic forces such as Germany's National Socialism in the 1930s, the university has historically been a powerful foe of demagoguery, totalitarianism, and the fads of the day. In this sense, it has been a balance wheel for society, both preserving the old and creating the new.

There is a tension in these two roles. The commitment to preservation of truth makes the university appear to some today as slow to adopt or even adapt to the new. For others, the commitment to create knowledge makes the university appear to reject our historic verities and the great canons of yesterday. However, as long as both the traditionalists and the progressives are each unhappy, perhaps the university is doing its job.

More familiar to most people than the repository role is the university's function as a transmitter of knowledge—the publishing, the collecting, the demonstrating, the broadcasting, the "websiting," and the teaching. All of these things are now being done by other educational providers as well—publishing companies, television networks, software makers, for-profit educators, and e-learning companies, to name a few. The university is different than every one of them in ways that should be prized.

The university is not market-driven in the manner that other for-profit educators must be. This means it does not give the public simply what it asks for, but also what the university believes the public needs. This must seem arrogant, but in plain English—or maybe just distilled academese—it translates into an organization that is not engaged only in vocational training, but instead in educating the whole person for a full life. At the risk of undermining my argument by referring to college catalogs, many speak of offering a liberal education that includes such things as cognitive development; emotional and ethical knowledge; preparation for citizenship and membership in a multicultural society; instruction related to family and community life; development of the taste and conduct needed to enjoy the good life; leisure use and health skills; development of personal traits such as leadership, coping, and adaptability; and, of course, preparation for productive work.

It is not surprising that universities do not accomplish all of these things. It is not even clear they do more than talk about some. However, they do achieve much that is desperately needed today. The half-life of knowledge is getting shorter and shorter. As a result, it is more important to provide students with a broad liberal education that teaches them how to think—creatively and critically—and to continuously learn throughout their lives than to give them the quickly dated vocational training necessary to get a first job. Study after study has shown that a liberal education makes not only educational sense, but also financial sense in terms of career progress and salary.

Moreover, universities are able to accomplish things other providers cannot. The new educational providers are focusing on instruction in high-enrollment areas requiring low-faculty involvement. This is the only way they can make money. For instance, at the graduate level, offering a masters degree in business administration is more profitable than a doctoral degree in physics. The reason is that the doctoral degree, which is of interest to a very small number of students, requires intense one-on-one involvement between a faculty member and a student. This is the most expensive brand of education there is. In contrast, the masters degree in business can be offered via large classes online or in person and has a very large potential student market. In addition, there are no state or national certification requirements for this degree, which means it can be offered worldwide.

Universities are likely to remain the sole source of education in low-enrollment undergraduate fields and in graduate education that relies on the apprenticeship model. This is not only the economic reality, but it is also the most desirable situation educationally. Universities are home to the most outstanding scholars in the world. These are the only people who can prepare the leading research scientists for tomorrow. It is because of this apprenticeship system that the U.S. holds the dominant position in scholarship in the world today. Despite complaints about graduate students teaching undergraduates or the unavailability of university faculty to students, which are serious problems that need to be addressed, our society benefits greatly from having our most renowned scholars teach and our university professors engage in scholarship. This is borne out not only in the many studies of student course evaluations that show that the highest teaching ratings go to the most productive scholars, but also in the continuing pre-eminence of the U.S. in preparing scholars.

SERVICE TO HUMANITY

Service can be described as the application of university research and expertise to addressing social problems. It is a historical accident—the result of the confluence of the creation of the first American research universities and the concurrent rise in the late 19th century of the Progressive Era with its focus on improving social conditions in the U.S. The two were somehow linked. This did not have to happen. The university could have been established as an ivory tower removed from society.

The service ideal is epitomized by the "Wisconsin Idea," an initiative launched by the University of Wisconsin during the first decade of the 20th century. University President Charles Van Hise sought to make the campus of the university the state of Wisconsin. This meant university assistance to government. Seemingly every branch of government had university faculty and administration experts working with them on a raft of issues varying from railroads and banks to natural resources and government regulation. It also meant that the university engaged in practical research on topics such as cow breeding and crop production and offered instruction to the citizens of the state on their farms, in their communities, on the campus, and via agricultural extension stations.

The service mission, although not as grandly conceived as at Wisconsin, was probably inevitable at other schools as well. Government would likely have demanded it in exchange for its funding of higher education. Also, as higher education grew from enrolling 4 percent of the college-age population in 1900 to more than 65 percent of high school graduates a century later, it would have been impossible for the university to have remained aloof or disconnected from the society.

Nonetheless, service is a gift, often a pro bono gift to society, but we have come to take it for granted as a responsibility of the university and the due of the society. Today every highly developed nation depends on the application of university research and expertise to address its social problems and to continue its advancement. However, no other educational provider engages in this activity. None can substitute for the university in providing it, and there are great limits to which the private sector and not-for-profit think tanks can fill the gap.

THE COMBINATION

The activities of the university are traditionally described as teaching, research, and service. At the majority of universities, only one of these activities, teaching or the transmission of knowledge, generates revenue. The money comes from tuition, not from creation, preservation, or application of knowledge. Research or creation is like college football: It is an income producer at a relatively small number of schools; the rest lose money.

For this reason, the new educational providers are only competing with traditional higher education in the area of teaching and they are only interested in the high-margin, high-volume fields. If nonuniversity educators make significant headway and manage to wrest important areas of instruction away from the university, they will leave higher education with the lower revenue, high-cost areas of instruction and the research and service functions. This combination is not financially viable because the university cannot support itself with these activities.

Even more important, it is not an intellectually viable combination either. There is a history of nations and higher education institutions that have separated research and teaching. The result is a feeble university staffed by pedagogues, teachers (not scholars) who are removed from cutting-edge research. The consequence is necessarily an arid and outdated curriculum. The quality of graduates—in knowledge of content and methods of advancing knowledge—is far poorer, particularly on the graduate level, than at institutions that join research and teaching.

One of the greatest risks we face as a nation in the growth of new educational providers is the unbundling of the teaching, research, and service functions. These functions are inextricably intertwined—the creation, preservation, dissemination, and application of knowledge. They should be regarded as indivisible in the sense that each informs, strengthens, and builds on the others. As teaching is weakened without linkage to knowledge creation, so too is knowledge creation without connection to preservation, and application uninformed by research. No modern society can afford to pay the enormous price that would be exacted should this combination be permitted to unravel.

CONCLUSIONS FOR THE NATION

It makes no sense for politicians to throw up their hands, as many seem to, when they talk about the university today. No modern democratic society has the option of turning its back on the university. The only real alternative is to embrace the university.

This should not be done uncritically. The university has a number of weaknesses and shortcomings, some of which were discussed earlier, that need improvement. The media, the government, and the business community should keep the public spotlight on these issues. The competition of new providers could be a means for fostering improvements in higher education, particularly with regard to serving and making education more accessible for students. Competition might even enhance the quality of instruction as some for-profits engage in teaching and learning assessment and take it more seriously than traditional universities. It could also provide examples of economies that higher education could adopt without reducing quality. Government might also use the competition between new and traditional providers to encourage such changes. Incentives for addressing the weaknesses could be powerful levers for action in critical areas such as improving the status of undergraduate education in research universities. So can disincentives and accountability measures that do not infringe on the principle of academic freedom in the university.

The American university is not only highly esteemed; it is also indispensable to our society. The task before us is not simply the maintenance but the nurturance of its essential functions—creation, preservation, transmission, and application of knowledge. Other organizations do engage in research, but we must remember the university is home to most of the basic and much of the applied research that the future of our country and the well-being of the world depends on. With regard to the preservation of knowledge, we must know that the university's function as a repository of knowledge is essential if there is to be a continuing neutral social critic for our society. With regard to the transmission of knowledge, we cannot forget that the university is the one educator that provides students with more than a market-driven education. It provides an education focusing not simply on the wants of the individual, but on the needs of the society, and preparation for membership in a democratic society. It also is the only educator of the scholars needed to fill the shoes of our current faculty and make the advances that will power tomorrow. With regard to the application of knowledge, the university is committed to the ethic of service to society in a way that no other social institution is or can be. Neither the for-profit sector, nor nonprofit knowledge organizations have the capacity or the desire to fill this role. With regard to all of these activities combined, we need to recognize that their unbundling would be a disaster not only for the university, but for society.

3

E-LEARNING IN THE POSTSECONDARY EDUCATION MARKET: A VIEW FROM WALL STREET

—*Greg Cappelli*
SENIOR EQUITY ANALYST FOR CREDIT SUISSE FIRST BOSTON

As much as many of us would like to hold on to the idealistic notion of a university operating outside the daily financial grind of revenues, expenses, and budgets, today's institutions of higher education are complex businesses. Indeed, as Arthur Levine noted in Chapter 2, "Higher Education," the state of higher education as an industry is being shaped profoundly by the fundamental economics of the business—labor, facilities, which courses are profitable, and which are not. Understanding the underlying business models behind the typical

41

nonprofit and for-profit institution is a prerequisite to thinking about the impact of a force such as e-learning.

Following the premise that as goes the money, so goes the industry, this chapter builds on Levine's discussion of the changes afoot in higher education to consider how they will impact the economics of the industry. As the senior equity research analyst at Wall Street giant Credit Suisse First Boston, Gregory Cappelli offers a view that is ironically seldom seen in traditional academe: how higher education institutions stack up as businesses. How many of us would describe the typical university as operating under an "airplane model"—the goal being to keep the seats full, leveraging fixed costs along the way?

Cappelli tackles e-learning's impact on higher education from a financial standpoint. After orienting us to the postsecondary industry's size and characteristics, he identifies some of the key changes the Internet has brought to other industries—lowered transaction costs, increased access to information, and redefinition of the limitations of space and time. Whereas Carol Twigg in Chapter 5 will tackle the question from the view of pedagogy and course redesign, Cappelli approaches the question by focusing on the key fundamental principles of how the economics underpinning the current model of higher education work and the impact that e-learning is likely to make as a result. He applies to universities the lessons learned from various industries that have experienced the ups and downs of being an "e"—e-travel, e-procurement, e-health, and so on—and as a result hones in on several unique prospects for change.

Cappelli is the Managing Director/Senior Analyst, U.S./Global Services/Education and e-learning, Credit Suisse First Boston (CSFB). He joined Credit Suisse First Boston in April 1997. He is a Managing Director and Senior Analyst responsible for heading the research coverage of CSFB's Global Services Team, including the Education and Technology/e-learning practices. Cappelli was ranked first place three years running (1998–2000) in the Institutional Investor All-America Research Teams in the Educational Services category. He also ranked first place in the 2000 Greenwich Associates survey of CEOs and CFOs. Greg has covered education and e-learning companies for more than seven years. He was recently selected to testify before the Senate Committee for the Web-based Education Commission Hearing in Washington, DC, and is frequently quoted in the press. Prior to joining CSFB, Cappelli was a Vice President and Senior Research Analyst with ABN AMRO. Cappelli holds an MBA in Finance from Dominican University, where he graduated with honors, and a BA in Economics from Indiana University.

The United States market for higher education is diverse and complex, driven by market forces, societal demands, and government policy. Over the past 30 years, postsecondary education has undergone many changes, and continues to do so, owing to shifting demographic trends, a movement toward greater numbers of nontraditional (older) students, higher tuition costs, and the increasing burden of personal debt through financial aid.

Against this backdrop, the question that organizes this book is one of transformation versus evolution. As an observer from Wall Street, to me the higher education market offers tremendous investment opportunities, ranging from distance-learning content providers, to e-learning enablers, to online student communities, to pure e-commerce companies. The trends that are shaping the broader *knowledge economy* are also taking place in higher education: mapping and measuring skill development against business models.

My firm, Credit Suisse First Boston, estimates the postsecondary education sector to be approximately 9 percent of the total for-profit industry, or $9 billion. The postsecondary market will remain a very attractive sector for the foreseeable future, offering a 15 percent compound annual growth rate (CAGR) over the next five years. Indeed, when compared to K–12 education and corporate training, I believe the higher education sector can take greatest advantage of the increased use of technology, especially the Internet, in delivering the educational product. Distance learning via the Internet will drive tremendous growth.

INCREASING ENROLLMENTS SHOULD DRIVE GROWTH

The National Center for Educational Statistics (NCES) is projecting a 20 percent increase in the number of high school graduates, from approximately 2.5 million in 1994 to 3.1 million in 2008, as children of the baby boom, or the echo boom, begin to graduate from high school (see Figure 3.1). This is likely to translate into increased enrollments at postsecondary institutions and increased demand

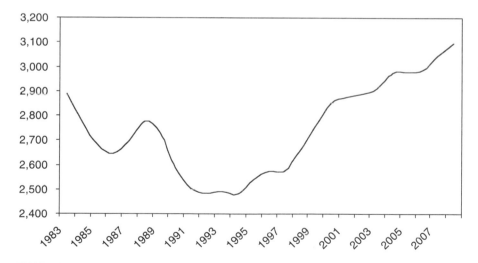

FIGURE 3.1
High School Graduates 1983–2008 (Total Number of High School Graduates; in Thousands). (*Source:* U.S. Department of Education, National Center for Education Statistics.)

for e-learning. The number of graduating high school seniors, which prior to 1995 had been declining over the previous 18 years, now serves as a tailwind for postsecondary educational institutions. In addition, the military continues to be less of a competitor, as cost-cutting programs have reduced the aggregate number of military personnel by nearly 36 percent since 1987.

The increased demand for adult higher education is compelling. More people are demanding college degrees and more high school graduates are choosing college. Approximately 68 percent of all 1998 high school graduates went on to college that same year, compared with 53 percent a decade ago. The number of adults enrolled in institutions of higher education programs in the United States is estimated by the NCES to reach 16 million by 2008 (see Figure 3.2). This is an important metric, as adult students are more likely to embrace distance learning as an acceptable means of education providing it contains the necessary content and credibility.

There are more than 15 million students enrolled in postsecondary institutions in the United States. Of the approximately 6,600 postsecondary schools eligible for Title IV funding, approximately 2,500 of them constitute the for-profit sector. On a combined basis, publicly traded for-profit higher education institutions currently enroll less than 10 percent of these students. There are significant opportunities for enrollment growth throughout the market for high-quality, brand name, for-profit education companies.

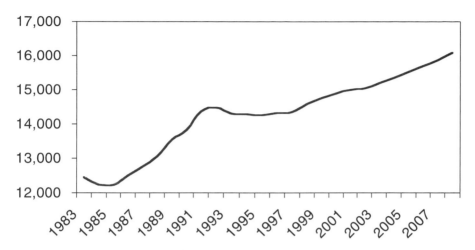

FIGURE 3.2
Total Projected Enrollments in Institutions of Higher Education (in Thousands). (*Source:* U.S. Department of Education, National Center for Education Statistics.)

According to the U.S. Department of Education, over 80 percent of college students are in public institutions (see Figure 3.3). These campuses are crowded and e-learning is uniquely positioned to relieve the pressure. The challenge they face is how best to deal with the expected influx of students when, in general, they are already overcrowded and overbudget. For many institutions the answer is expansion of e-learning initiatives. As distance learning takes off, it may relieve the pressure on our nation's higher education system.

As the United States is transformed into a knowledge economy, demand has increased for education and skilled workers. As such, a higher number of older, nontraditional students are investing in education. Many of these students

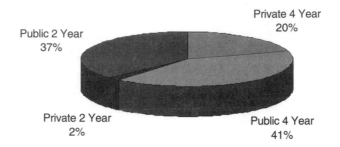

FIGURE 3.3
Total U.S. Postsecondary Enrollment (As a Percent of Total Postsecondary Enrollment, Projected 1998). (*Source:* U.S. Department of Education, National Center for Education Statistics.)

are working adults who have limited free time. Because of the demands placed on them by their employers, they are turning to distance learning to solve both their need for education and their time constraints.

Demographic projections suggest that, from 1985 to 2005, there is likely to be a 70 percent increase of the number of people aged 35 and older seeking postsecondary education. Although this percentage increase seems unusually large, I should point out that the student base in this age bracket is relatively small. The NCES estimated that by 1999, the number of adults enrolled in higher education programs in the United States would reach approximately 7 million people (see Figure 3.4).

Demographers anticipated that approximately 43 percent of an estimated 16 million students enrolled in higher education institutions in the year 2000 would be over the age of 24, and that 70 percent to 75 percent of them would

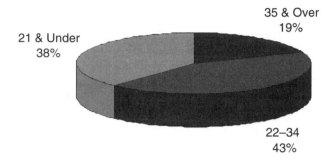

FIGURE 3.4
Enrollment in Higher Education Institutions (by Age). (*Source:* U.S. Department of Education, National Center for Education Statistics.)

be employed. The adult age cohort is the fastest growing segment of students in postsecondary education. Although the number of high school graduates likely will have a substantial effect on the growth of institutions of higher learning over the next decade, the growth of the number of working adults returning to school is likely to be just as significant. For many of the reasons already mentioned, e-learning is well situated to address the educational needs of working adults.

EXPENDITURES SUPPORT E-LEARNING GROWTH

We live in a world of advanced technology that has placed new demands on employers and employees, resulting in the need for a more technically trained population. Public and private institutions of higher education must continue to adapt to these demands. As an observer from Wall Street, it is clear to me that where there is change, there is opportunity. Postsecondary education is clearly an area where select e-learning for-profit companies can capitalize on the increased demand for lifelong learning.

Throughout the 1990s, there was a general push toward privatization of a broad range of services. Postsecondary education has been at the center of many policy issues, and public institutions are likely to become the target of tax cuts and the victims of increasing competition for state funds. As the cost of education has continued to rise, federal and state appropriations have decreased, causing many state schools to cut instruction, programs, and infrastructure, even in the face of a growing base of students.

As a result, it was only a matter of time before the private, for-profit enterprise leaders began to realize the inefficiencies in the system for higher education and began to offer a redefined product designed with the demands of contemporary students in mind. This pattern is demonstrated by the growth in expenditures in the higher education sector (see Figure 3.5). High-quality, convenient, and cost-effective postsecondary education is the hallmark of successful for-profit education companies. If you believe that the system for postsecondary education is in need of improvement, then this need presents opportunities to for-profit institutions, such as e-learning companies, to deliver improved educational outcomes.

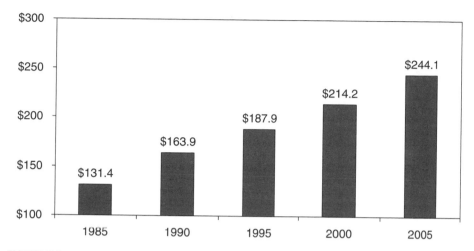

FIGURE 3.5
Growth of Expenditures on Higher Education ($ in Billions). (*Source:* U.S. Department of Education, National Center for Education Statistics.)

According to data from the U.S. Department of Education, aggregate revenue for institutions of higher education was slightly over $208 billion in 1998. This is up almost 60 percent since 1985 and is projected to increase another 30 percent by 2005. However, the revenue and expenditure statistics illustrate that state and federal funding of postsecondary education has been decreasing and that students enrolled in public postsecondary institutions are footing a greater proportion of the tuition bill to offset the loss of taxpayer support. While federal, state, and local governments continue to divert tax dollars toward other social priorities, the cost of education is shifting from taxpayers to students. Students are increasingly likely to search out the schools that will offer them the best return on their investment. For-profit e-learning companies can address the educational needs of many students, as they focus on disciplines with economic value and are more flexible in terms of scheduling and convenience.

In addition, technology and education are converging at a rapid pace. Institutions are aggressively spending money on technology. Information technology (IT) spending by higher education institutions is projected to increase over 50 percent between 1998 and 2003 to $4.8 billion (see Figure 3.6). This 9 percent annual growth in technology spending will be driven by a number of factors, including an increasing number of schools and total enrollments, ad-

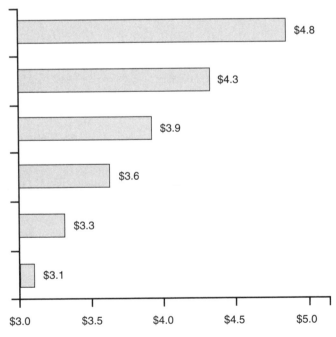

FIGURE 3.6
Total IT Spending by U.S. Higher Education Institutions 1998–2003 ($ in Billions). (*Source:* U.S. Department of Education, National Center for Education Statistics.)

vances in new technologies, the changing needs of students, and the rollout of e-learning programs. As postsecondary institutions continue to add to their distance-learning course offerings, certain e-learning companies, particularly the enablers, should expect to see an increased demand for their products and services.

DISTANCE LEARNING IN POSTSECONDARY EDUCATION

Distance learning is becoming increasingly popular in higher education. Enrollments in distance learning totaled 700,000 in 1998. This number is projected to grow at a 35 percent CAGR to 2.2 million students in 2002 (see Figure 3.7). The strong growth will be the result of the better technological-based platforms becoming an inexpensive means for delivering high-quality educational courses and content.

The number of students enrolled in distance education as a percentage of total postsecondary enrollments is projected to triple to almost 15 percent in 2002 from just 5 percent in 1998 (see Figure 3.8).

The figure for enrollment in distance education demonstrates the projected rise in the percentage of colleges offering distance learning. Clearly, the number of colleges offering distance learning is growing at a rapid pace at both two-year

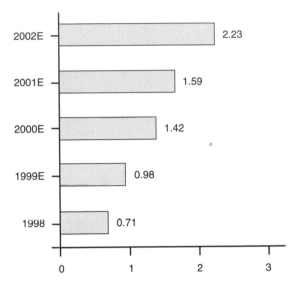

FIGURE 3.7
Enrollments in Postsecondary Distance Education (in Millions). (*Source:* U.S. Department of Education, National Center for Education Statistics.)

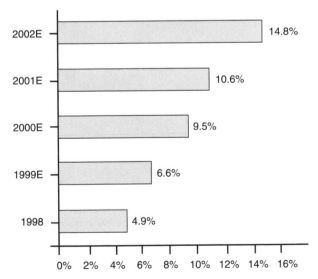

FIGURE 3.8
Enrollments in Distance Education (As a Percent of Total Postsecondary Enrollment). (*Source:* U.S. Department of Education, National Center for Education Statistics.)

and four-year institutions (see Figure 3.9). Interestingly, the projected growth in distance learning course offerings is greater for two-year institutions than it is for four-year institutions despite traditionally heavier spending by four-year schools. According to IDC, four-year institutions spent approximately $160,000 on distance learning versus approximately $75,000 by two-year institutions in 1999. However, two-year schools have been spending more on hardware, software, and communication products as a percentage of overall expenditures, which might indicate that two-year schools are quickly building the infrastructure necessary to expand distance-learning offerings. Distance-learning expen-

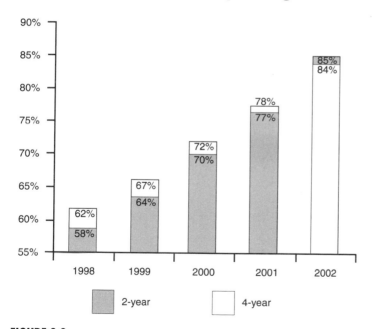

FIGURE 3.9

Colleges Offering Distance Learning (As a Percent of Total Institutions of Higher Learning). (*Source:* U.S. Department of Education, National Center for Education Statistics.)

ditures may benefit two-year schools more than others as they generally have fewer students living on campus.

Furthermore, the data suggests that growth will be even more prevalent in public four-year institutions. According to IDC, public institutions will spend twice as much on distance learning than private institutions, which will be the result of larger enrollments and less emphasis on one-on-one attention. The areas most likely to support this growth across all schools (public/private, two-year/four-year) are business, computer science, English, Foreign Language, and Graduate and Postgraduate studies departments.

As the topic of this book suggests, the Internet is the most widely used technology vehicle for distance-learning courses. The Internet's easy-to-use interface and interactivity make it a natural vehicle for distance learning. Based on a survey by IDC, 78 percent of the higher education institutions that offer distance learning used the Internet. The next highest ranked technology was videotape, at 59 percent (see Figure 3.10).

As a result of the self-paced nature of distance-learning, the education content is usually organized differently than traditional in-class methods. Distance learning content is organized in such a way that information can reach all types of learners through different types of media. Traditional textbook material must be augmented with multimedia and graphical interfaces to reach those learners who need visual or oral communication to retain the information.

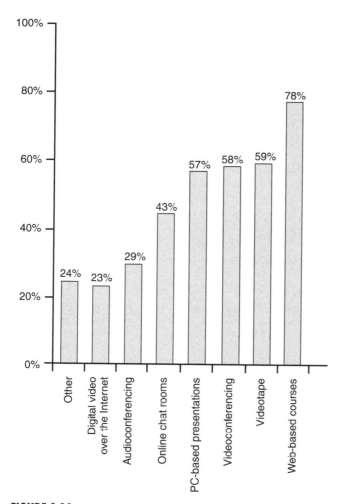

FIGURE 3.10
Distance-Learning Technologies in Use at Higher Education Institutions, 1998. (*Source:* U.S. Department of Education, National Center for Education Statistics.)

Distance-learning courses are often less structured than traditional in-class courses. As a result, the student can switch media easily and often to better suit a desired or more effective learning method. For example, if a student cannot understand the textbook readings, he or she can switch to the Internet or multimedia presentation for a different perspective. However, in doing so, the student must be guided carefully on the necessary outcomes of each lesson as he or she does not have an instructor stressing the key points of each learning session.

FORCES DRIVING DISTANCE LEARNING

Traditional students in higher education come directly from high school and are not necessarily committed to gaining their education in the shortest time possible. The traditional higher education student is between the ages of 18 to 23 and is attending college largely because he or she knows a degree is important in the abstract. Most, however, are uncertain of their long-term aspirations or how a specific degree will ultimately help them. This traditional student is a somewhat unpredictable learner and takes a reactive, rather than proactive, approach to education. The profile of a distance learner appears to be remarkably different from the traditional student. The Department of Education estimates that the average distance learner is 26 or older and female. This nontraditional distance education student is an active learner and can absorb educational content easily in almost any form. Although some forms are better suited to certain students, the average distance learner is quite open to different delivery methods and content styles. The prototypical distance learner is someone who cannot easily commit to a rigid class schedule, such as working adults, working parents, disabled students, school teachers, or military personnel. However, traditional students will quickly be converted to online learning as technology improves and learning outcomes continue to increase.

The initial pioneers in the distance education market were community colleges and public universities, where there is an emphasis on public service. Now, the majority of colleges and universities offer (or will soon introduce) distance-learning courses to better serve their existing or potential student bodies and to penetrate a wider potential student base. Owing to the early success of the public colleges and universities and improved technologies, for-profit institutions have begun to enter the distance education market. For-profit education companies are using distance learning as a way of reaching out to a larger student base, reducing per-student costs, increasing enrollment, and reducing students' time and travel constraints. These factors will likely continue to drive enrollment growth in the distance-learning segment of the for-profit education market. However, this overwhelming increase in demand is also likely to continue to attract market competition.

DISTANCE LEARNING BENEFICIAL TO BRICKS-AND-MORTAR EDUCATION

In addition to creating a larger potential student body, distance learning offers for-profit education companies the opportunity for margin expansion. By leveraging their available content across a wider platform and lower per-student cost base, distance education can be a very attractive alternative to traditional bricks-and-mortar schools. However, offsetting this margin improvement is the fact that developing and delivering distance education programs is not as easy as it sounds. Companies involved with distance-learning usually have to invest in a greater level of customer service for their students, as these are students that can "get lost in the system" if a school fails to deliver its distance students the appropriate amount of attention. To some extent, this could potentially limit the growth rate for certain degree-granting distance-learning companies, as quality versus quantity must be the overriding factor when rolling out these programs. In any case, at this time, experience suggests that the average for-profit school has significantly higher margins in its distance education courses owing to the low incremental cost per additional student. In addition, this margin gap may continue to rise as online courses gain operating leverage through increased enrollments and less expensive technology.

ONLINE COMMUNITIES IN POSTSECONDARY EDUCATION

Although perhaps out of fashion to argue since the dot-com bust, e-learning may bring with it a significant e-commerce opportunity. Nearly 15 million U.S. college students account for more than $100 billion in annual spending. As previously stated, these students are particularly attractive to advertisers because they are at an age where they develop lifelong brand loyalties, increasing the benefits of advertising. There has already been significant competition to capture this elusive Web traffic. However, e-learning is an ideal candidate for online communities, as over 95 percent of college students are already on the Web. A successful online community should be greatly rewarded by this group's enormous e-commerce and advertising prospects.

According to a recent survey, almost half of all students and teachers use the Internet at least once a day (see Figures 3.11 and 3.12). The penetration rate has increased substantially over the last five years, from only 8 percent in 1994 to 44 percent in 1998. Clearly, the Internet is a part of everyday life for teachers and students, creating significant opportunities for e-learning companies that can provide content-rich, easy-to-use Web portals.

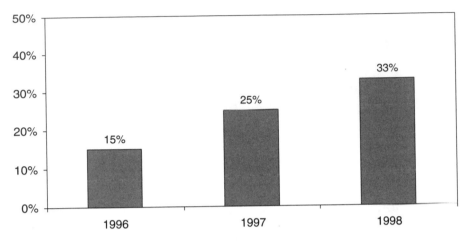

FIGURE 3.11
College Classes Using Internet Resources (Percent of Classes Using the Internet as Part of Curriculum). (*Source:* The 1998 National Survey of Information Technology in Higher Education.)

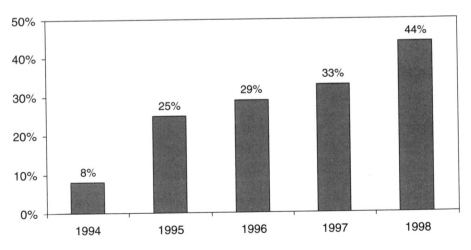

FIGURE 3.12
College Students and Teachers Connected to the Web (Percent of Students and Teachers Who Use the Internet at Least Once a Day). (*Source:* The 1998 National Survey of Information Technology in Higher Education and Credit Suisse First Boston.)

The number of online college students is even greater, rising from 42 percent in 1996 to 95 percent and over 12 million students by 2003. For several reasons this is a positive for proprietary educational product and service providers as the college market represents an enormous opportunity. As previously noted, there are more than 1.4 million people enrolled in higher education distance education. The number of students online and enrolled in online courses will continue to grow, resulting in large increases in overall expenditures. I do not see immediate deterioration in pricing power for online providers, as the average price per course for online courses is generally comparable to traditional brick-and-mortar courses. According to the U.S. Department of Education, 57 percent of institutions are charging both comparable tuition and comparable fees for distance education and on-campus courses. Furthermore, I have yet to see significant signs of cannibalization, as schools that offer online courses generally offer them to supplement traditional courses rather than as a replacement. However, as distance learning increases in popularity, I would expect to see more courses offered only via the Internet.

4

THE EMERGING GLOBAL E-EDUCATION INDUSTRY

—*Martin Irvine*
GEORGETOWN UNIVERSITY

No consideration of the industry-level impact that e-learning is making in higher education would be complete without explicitly considering its global context. It has long been said—with good reason—that the United States system of higher education is the envy of the world. In terms of access, size, and quality, few question the leadership role that the U.S. has played in shaping the face of postsecondary education (albeit having assimilated traditions mostly formed around the globe centuries ago). Similar U.S.-centric chest pounding has been known in the information technology (IT) industry as well.

For these reasons, the growth of e-learning is too often considered only in a domestic context. Yet at its core, the Internet is a global network and the flow of supply and demand for postsecondary education across the world offers a tremendous opportunity for e-learning. Whether one considers challenges as big as the dearth of access to brick-and-mortar campuses in Africa and China, or as simple as the cost and inconvenience of exchange programs with students who desire access to U.S. educational programs, the potential benefits and uses of e-learning become clear.

The degree to which e-learning's impact on higher education is transformative or evolutionary will, in large measure, depend on how it scales globally. Will Australian universities become a dominant provider of courses to southeast Asia? Will "traditional" education in the U.S. include courses from institutions abroad? Will a small number of institutions dominate the postsecondary education industry by taking on a global "franchise" model, opening branch campuses around the world? The answers to these questions are not solely based on e-learning, but they are heavily influenced by the breaking down of traditional barriers to global access to higher education. Institutions such as the Open University and Sylvan International Universities may not be household names to many, but their global modus operandi may have profound implications for how tomorrow's undergraduate might think about his or her college options.

Naturally, it is difficult to reduce a discussion of world-wide higher education into a single chapter. Nevertheless, Georgetown University professor Martin Irvine tackles this Herculean task well. He explores the size and trends that characterize the global higher education market, tying in the influence of e-learning along the way. If the balance of this book opens the reader's eyes to the profound influence e-learning is having in the U.S., Irvine's review of the global landscape will reveal an even grander context for change abroad.

Martin Irvine is the Founding Director of the graduate program in Communication, Culture & Technology (CCT) and Associate Vice President for Technology Strategy at Georgetown University. He has been involved in the Internet and higher education for 10 years.

Martin received his BA from the State University of New York at Buffalo and his PhD from Harvard University. He began his interest in computing at Harvard, and he became the first PhD in a liberal arts field at Harvard to write a dissertation on a computer (in 1982). Irvine has been a professor at Georgetown since 1988, and has also taught at Harvard, Wayne State University, and the University of Virginia. His guide to the Web for students, Web Works, *was published by W.W. Norton in 1996.*

Irvine has been a technology entrepreneur within higher education since 1993. The CCT Program, founded in 1995, was the first Internet-centered, multidisciplinary graduate program devoted to preparing students for careers in the information economy (see cct.georgetown.edu). As Associate Vice President for Technology Strategy at Georgetown, Irvine works to advance the use of enabling technologies in the university's core mission of teaching and research, and to establish external partnerships with technology companies.

Irvine was a founding director of the Washington, DC, Technology Council, and he continues to serve on its Board of Directors. Irvine was also a cofounder and director of Incube8, an Internet business development company based in Baltimore. He's also a business advisor for Paras Ventures, a venture network based in Washington, DC.

His current initiatives involve e-learning and developing the information architecture and business models for distance education on the Internet. He is currently writing a book, Net Knowledge: The Coming Revolution in Higher Education, *an analysis of the higher education industry and its future in the post-Internet era.*

The growth in the number of people entering postsecondary education and the sharply rising global demand for education through globalization and the knowledge economy have created the market conditions for a truly global education industry. From 1950 to 1997, enrollments in postsecondary education worldwide increased from 6.5 million in 1950 to 88.2 million in 1997, and they have been forecast to reach 160 million by 2025.[1] As noted in Chapter 3, "E-Learning in the Postsecondary Education Market," by Greg Cappelli, postsecondary education represents a $250-billion industry in the U.S. alone, and a substantial part of world education expenditures goes to this sector. In short, the global education marketplace represents an extraordinary opportunity. However, given the disparities and constraints in resources found throughout the world, there are clearly challenges that create risks for the development of the industry on a global scale.

As for the question of transformation versus evolution, the Internet offers revolutionary potential for the global higher education market. To begin, demand for education worldwide has never been greater, especially in developing countries. At the same time, the resources for education are often nonexistent in many parts of the world. Government funds for education are insufficient to meet demand even in wealthy countries. Education has traditionally been a jealously guarded local and national matter and a solidifier of cultural differences, approached more in social and cultural terms than in the terms of business models and markets. Whereas national economies are linked by international exchanges of goods, services, and investments, and by cross-border flows of money, communications, and intellectual property in electronic networks, the idea that education is part of a global, networked knowledge economy is only now becoming a common working assumption. However, the economic and social effects of education are now clearly driving the worldwide adoption of e-learning and e-education services.

Peter Stokes, Executive Vice President of Eduventures, observed in a recent industry white paper that the global networked economy is creating new drivers for education, and that "sustaining growth among regional communities will depend upon a successful shift away from commodities-based economies toward the development of knowledge-based economies. In this way, education is becoming a truly international concern. As a result, demand for new kinds of learning opportunities is increasing across communities on a worldwide basis."[2]

Recent analyses of the education industry, which include factors such as the growth of the for-profit education sector, universities expanding into e-learning, U.S. universities opening satellite campuses abroad, and an explosion of technology companies and education content providers indicate the huge worldwide market opportunity—as high as $2 trillion, in Merrill Lynch's often-cited estimation of the total global market.[3] Regardless of our ability to size accurately the global market at the macro level, it is clear that we have seen important new developments that were not around 10 years ago, developments that now clearly define the future trajectory of the industry.

The first such development is the emergence of a global business network serving the education marketplace. This industry network now includes publishers (paper and digital), media companies, software and hardware companies, Internet and communication services, for-profit and nonprofit education providers, and consulting services and integrators, just to name a few.[4] The second development is an aspect of globalization found in the movement toward international or transnational education standards and the new business models of private-sector education providers. This development can be seen both in major nongovernmental organization (NGO) studies of the economic role of private education and in actual global market advances by companies such as Sylvan, the National Institute for Information Technology (NIIT), based in India and now in 20 other countries, and the new Thomson-Universitas 21 joint venture (a partnership formed from an alliance of universities around the world and a major private-sector education company).

The global education industry, of course, is a huge topic. For this industry overview, I focus on the following major issues:

1. Global education economics and the growth of the private sector.

2. The marketplace realities for global e-learning:

- Demographics of world participation in post-secondary education.
- The readiness of the world market for the emerging industry.
- The language populations in the marketplace.

3. Education and e-learning as international trade.
4. The technology infrastructure and access barriers to global education.

I conclude with case studies of global e-learning businesses, considering a range of possible business models involving universities, private-sector education providers and joint ventures, and NGO economic development.

EDUCATION ECONOMICS AND THE GROWTH OF THE PRIVATE SECTOR

In terms of the economics of education, approximately 63 percent of all education costs worldwide are met by governments, and much of the growing e-learning industry will be based on sales to state-funded organizations. Although education remains predominantly publicly funded, the private sector is becoming increasingly more important and accounts for 35 percent of worldwide education funding.

Average levels of total spending on education worldwide have remained around 5 percent of gross national product (GNP) for more developed countries and 4 percent for less developed countries in the period between 1980 and 1997.[5] The economic impact and multiplier effects of education are also main drivers for worldwide interest in expanding education access through e-learning. In the U.S., every dollar spent on education returns $5 to the economy. A World Bank study in 1990 showed that an increase of one year in the average length of education in a country could lead to a 3 percent rise in gross domestic product (GDP).[6]

The worldwide education marketplace is seeing changes in ownership and the provision of education from childhood through adulthood. There are several drivers behind the shift to increased private-sector education provision: School-age populations are increasing and adult populations now need life-long learning; governments cannot increase funding to meet demand; growing middle-class populations can afford the cost of education; and corporations worldwide need skilled workers. The global education marketplace is primed for huge growth as more governments and organizations open markets for private and for-profit providers to meet education needs where public funds cannot. The growth of North American for-profit higher education companies such as Sylvan, Strayer, DeVry, Thomson, and University of Phoenix in responding to education market needs is well known in the industry, but similar developments in private education companies are occurring worldwide. Recent studies by James Tooley and the World Bank's EdVest group have shown that many nations, especially in the developing world, have seen great advancements in access to education and economic growth through private education companies.[7] Private education companies, both for-profit and nonprofit, have stepped in to fill a demand for quality education in many areas where state provision is lacking.

The emerging data on private postsecondary education spending is impressive, indicating future growth in the sector. An estimated 40 percent of total education spending in Chile, Peru, the Philippines, and Thailand is privately funded.[8] The Philippines and Japan both have 76 percent of their students in private higher education schools. Figure 4.1 provides examples of private postsecondary enrollment worldwide.

The worldwide education sector also includes companies that manage "chains" of schools and universities, sometimes on a franchise basis, that are able to benefit from economies of scale. The largest of these, Objetivo/UNIP, is one of several competing chains of private schools in Brazil. It has more than 500,000 students from kindergarten to university in nearly 500 campuses. Educor, of South Africa, listed on the Johannesburg Stock Exchange, has more than 300,000 students. The company provides education services from high school to professional and vocational studies.

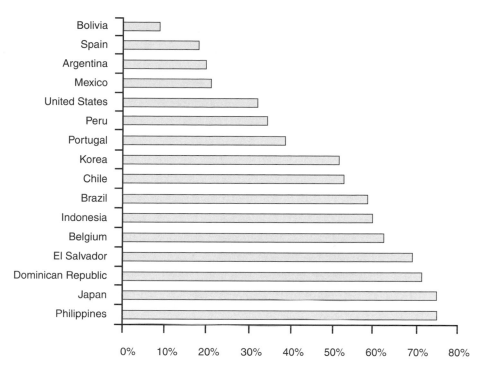

FIGURE 4.1
World Enrollment in Postsecondary Education, Various Nations. (*Source:* World Bank, EdInvest Data.)

India-based NIIT has 400,000 vocational and academic students in India and 20 other countries, including the United States. What is surprising, when considered from the dominant public-sector education policy perspective, is that the majority of the private education companies serve students from the whole income and demographic range and are generally regarded as high-quality with strong brand-name recognition.[9] The private institutions and for-profit education providers are both meeting market needs and creating new business webs for a global education industry.

MARKETPLACE REALITIES: WORLD PARTICIPATION IN POSTSECONDARY EDUCATION

Companies in the e-learning market doing business in the U.S. can rely on general industry homogeneity, known regulations and standards, reliable demographics and economic data, and reliable infrastructures. This is not the case outside the U.S. As Nagi Sioufi, CEO of the French language training software firm Auralog, put it, "There is not one international education market. There is an accumulation of local markets."[10] Entry into the global marketplace requires local knowledge, local partners, and focused market research.

Making a truly global education marketplace a reality, not just in developed countries, will take many years. Achieving even universal primary education worldwide, an obvious precondition for a postsecondary industry, will prove to be an enormous challenge, even with combined private and public investments. UNESCO Assistant Director-General John Daniel, the former Vice-Chancellor of Britain's Open University, recently estimated that 15 million more teachers are needed to achieve universal basic education by 2015, a goal pledged by more than 180 governments. Getting to the point of a global marketplace of people prepared for Internet-enabled, postsecondary education will take decades for many nations to accomplish.

TABLE 4–1 World Participation in Postsecondary Education
(Enrollment and Gross Enrollment Ratios in Tertiary Education, 1997)

	1997 ENROLLMENT (IN MILLIONS)			1997 GROSS ENROLLMENT RATIO		
	M/F*	F*	%F*	M/F	M	F
World Total	**88.2**	**41.3**	**47.0**	**17.4**	**18.1**	**16.7**
More developed regions	34.2	17.9	52.0	61.1	56.8	65.6
Northern America	16.0	8.9	55.0	80.7	70.8	91.0
Asia/Oceania	5.5	2.5	46.0	42.1	43.3	40.9
Europe	12.7	6.5	52.0	50.7	47.9	53.6
Countries in transition	11.0	6.0	54.0	34.0	30.6	37.6
Less developed regions	43.0	17.4	40.0	10.3	12.0	8.5
Sub-Saharan Africa	2.2	0.8	35.0	3.9	5.1	2.8
Arab states	3.9	1.6	41.0	14.9	17.3	12.4
Latin America/Caribbean	9.4	4.5	48.0	19.4	20.1	18.7
Eastern Asia/Oceania	16.8	6.8	41.0	10.8	12.5	9.0
China	6.1	2.0	33.0	6.1	7.8	4.2
Southern Asia	9.3	3.2	34.0	7.2	9.1	5.1
India	6.4	2.3	36.0	7.2	8.8	5.5
Least developed countries	1.9	0.5	27.0	3.2	4.6	1.7

Source: UNESCO World Education Report, 2000.[11] Gross education data represents all levels of enrollment, including students beyond the traditional age group, and partly measures education system capacity. Gross ratios may exceed 100 percent.

*M/F Male/Female; F Female; %F Female Percentage

Before considering the market potential, we need reliable data for understanding the size of the postsecondary global marketplace based on the number of people actually prepared for these services. What does the current marketplace look like demographically? Table 4–1 shows the major demographics on world participation in postsecondary (tertiary) education. Computer and Internet-enabled education and e-learning are motivated by the urgent need in developing countries to close the education gap with the rich nations. According to UNESCO data, only about 3.9 percent of people in sub-Saharan Africa and 7.2 percent in Southern Asia currently attend some form of postsecondary education. This compares with 58 percent in industrialized countries and 81 percent in North America. The correlation of education and developed nation status could not be clearer.

With only 17 percent of the world's adults participating in some form of tertiary (postsecondary) education, e-learning is rapidly being embraced as the only way to scale ongoing education to the world of need. In 1990, there were 48 million people in higher education worldwide. By 2025, the market could grow to 160 million, according to Thomson Learning and other analysts. As a result, education delivered with business-as-usual approaches is totally unviable. As Alan Gilbert, the head of Universitas 21, noted, "The possibility of traditional institutions meeting this demand is nil."[12] The challenge to the e-learning industry is capturing the opportunity with enough combined resources to meet the needs of the marketplace in all its cultural diversity.

READINESS OF THE WORLD MARKET

Preparedness for postsecondary education varies widely across world education markets. Indicators such as adult

TABLE 4–2 Social Factors and Population Preparation for Postsecondary Education

	Estimated Adult Literacy Rate, 1997 (%)			Gross Secondary Education Enrollment Ratios, 1997 (as %)			Telephone Main Lines (per thousand inhabitants)		Number of PCs (per thousand inhabitants)
	M/F*	M*	F*	M/F	M	F	1990	1997	1997
World Total	**78.1**	**84.1**	**72.2**	**60.1**	**64.0**	**56.0**	**97**	**139**	**58**
More developed regions	98.6	99.1	98.1	108.0	107.0	109.2	466	554	274
North America				98.2	97.8	98.6	537	633	388
Asia/Oceania				102.4	102.6	102.1	441	482	223
Europe				113.2	111.6	114.9	424	521	204
Countries in transition				87.0	85.4	88.6	126	180	35
Less developed regions	71.5	79.5	63.4	51.6	56.6	46.3	21	54	12
Sub-Saharan Africa	58.2	66.7	50.1	26.2	29.1	23.3	10	15	8
Arab states	58.5	70.6	45.9	56.9	61.2	52.3	33	55	10
Latin America/Caribbean	87.5	88.5	86.4	62.2	59.2	65.3	61	107	31
Eastern Asia/Oceania	84.3	91.1	77.3	66.3	69.3	63.1	18	64	13
China	82.2	90.3	73.7	70.1	73.7	66.2	6	57	6
Southern Asia	53.2	64.8	41.0	45.3	54.1	35.8	7	22	2
India	54.9	66.5	42.5	49.1	59.1	38.2	6	18	2
Least developed countries	48.4	58.9	38.0	19.3	23.5	15.0	3	4	1

Note: World literacy rates for developed nations include countries in transition as an aggregate. Gross secondary education data represents all levels of enrollment, including students beyond the traditional age group, and partly measures education system capacity. Gross ratios may exceed 100 percent.

Source: UNESCO World Education Report, 2000.[13]

*M/F Male/Female; F Female; %F Female Percentage

**M/F Male/Female; M* Male Percentage

literacy rates, secondary education completion, access to computers, and telephone lines shows continued concentration in the developed world. Telecommunications access and PC ownership have increased since 1997, but the pattern is clear (see Table 4–2).

The earliest markets for global e-education will obviously be in regions with a concentration of people prepared for postsecondary education with high usage of PCs and what is known as *teledensity* (concentration of telecom systems). In some countries, education is actually driving the adoption of computers and the Internet, a move that will create economic growth and a new business environment.

LANGUAGE COMMUNITIES ONLINE AND MARKET POSITION OF ENGLISH LANGUAGE INSTRUCTION

Although English remains the language used most on the Internet and the de facto standard for business and scientific communications, by 2005, non-English speakers will become the majority of Internet users. A recent report by the United Nations World Intellectual Property Organization (WIPO) indicates that by 2007 Chinese will surpass English as the most used language on the Internet.[14] Until recently, Internet domain names have been issued mostly in English and Roman characters around the world, but now domain names are being registered in Chinese, Japanese, Russian, and Arabic. With stronger language and national identities accompanying Internet globalization, a huge market demand for education content and services will follow the growth in non-English language communities on the Web.

In the near term, Asian and Spanish language markets will remain the fastest growing, and education services need to be customized for these language groups. Although Australia is currently the leader in e-learning services and revenues in the Pacific region (excluding Japan), International Data Corp. (IDC) projects that China and Korea will lead the region in e-learning by 2005.[15]

Figure 4.2 shows current language distribution on the Internet, but the rapid growth in Chinese Internet users makes language demographics a quickly moving target. Table 4–3 shows a more detailed distribution of language communities on the Internet and an indication of the complexity of the world education marketplace when the language of instruction is a factor in deploying services and content.

Education companies and universities are now creating content and programs in multiple languages, also looking to the huge demand for English language instruction using online and offline methods. Companies like Sylvan and Universitas 21 see their first market entry points in Asia and in Spanish-speaking countries, markets with most of the right conditions for providing large-scale education services.

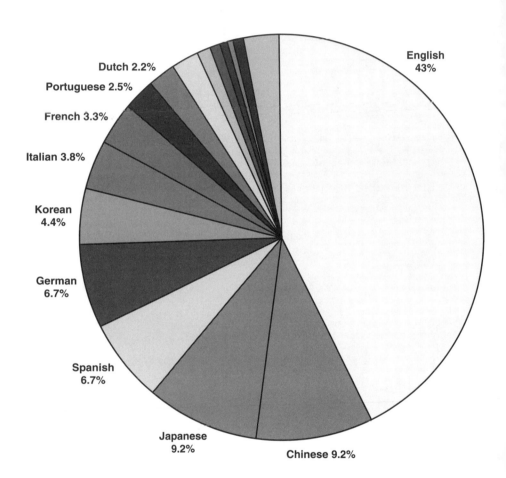

FIGURE 4.2

Major Online Language Populations. (*Source:* Global Reach, September 2001 Data.)[16]

TABLE 4–3 Global Market by Language Use, Language Community, and Economics, 2001

	INTERNET ACCESS (M)	% WORLD ONLINE POPULATION 2001	ESTIMATED ONLINE IN 2003 (M)	TOTAL POPULATION (M)	GDP ($B)	% OF WORLD ECONOMY	GDP PER CAPITA (1,000s)	NET HOSTS
English	220.4	43.0%	270	860	$13,812	33.4%		
Non-English	292.7	57.0%	505	5,340	$27,590	66.6%		
European	163.0	31.8%	290	1,089	$12,550	30.3%		
Languages (non-English)								
Catalan	0.7		8					
Czech	1.0		3	10.3	$53		$5.1	113
Dutch	11.1	2.2%	12.8	23.6	$570		$24.2	1,622
Finnish	2.3		4	5.2	$127		$24.4	772
French	16.8	3.3%	30	80.7	$1,734	4.2%	$21.5	1,996
German	34.2	6.7%	46	97.2	$2,421	5.8%	$24.9	2,999
Greek	1.5		3	10.9	$184		$16.9	148
Hungarian	1.3		3	10.1	$96		$9.4	159
Italian	19.5	3.8%	25	59.6	$1,471	3.6%	$24.7	1,653
Polish	3.1		6	39.4	$306		$7.8	372
Portuguese	12.8	2.5%	26	176.4	$1,472	3.6%	$8.34	1,055
Romanian	0.6			22.4	$98		$4.4	41
Russian	9.3	1.8%	15	144	$730	1.8%	$5.0	360
Danish	2.9			5.4	$176		$32.9	436
Icelandic	0.14			.3	$6		$23.5	44
Norwegian	2.5			4.6	$126		$27.7	525

TABLE 4–3 Global Market by Language Use, Language Community, and Economics, 2001 (continued)

	INTERNET ACCESS (M)	% WORLD ONLINE POPULATION 2001	ESTIMATED ONLINE IN 2003 (M)	TOTAL POPULATION (M)	GDP ($B)	% OF WORLD ECONOMY	GDP PER CAPITA (1,000s)	NET HOSTS
Swedish	5.6			10	$223		$22.3	764
Scandinavian languages (total)	11.1	2.2%	12.2	20.2	$525	1.3%	$26.0	1,769
Slovak	0.7		1	5.4	$47		$8.7	37
Slovenian	0.46		1	1.9	$22.9		$10.9	24
Spanish	34.6	6.7%	60	336.5	$3,684	8.9%	$11.0	1,731
Turkish	2.2		3	67.4	$454		$6.7	114
Ukrainian	0.7		2	50.3	$115		$2.3	34
Total European Languages (excl. English)	163.0	31.8%	290	1,162.4	$14,112	34.1%		14,965
Asian Languages								
Arabic	4.1	0.9%	6	162	$678	1.6%	$4.2	51
Chinese	47.5	9.2%	160	988	$5,370	13.0%	$5.4	2,345
Hebrew	1.0			6.3	$132		$21.0	180
Japanese	47.3	9.2%	75	127	$3,315	8.0%	$26.1	4,640
Korean	22.7	4.4%	35	47.9	$835	2.0%	$17.3	398
Malay	4.7			229	$835	2.0%	$3.7	121
Thai	2.3			62.4	$453		$7.3	63
Total Asian	129.5	25.3%	270					
Total World	505		793	6,200	$41,400			7,789

Source: Global Reach, Global Internet Usage by Language Group.[17]

EDUCATION AND E-LEARNING AS INTERNATIONAL TRADE

Education and training are the fifth-largest traded service in the United States, with international students contributing more than $11 billion to the U.S. economy. The number of international students attending colleges and universities in the United States increased by 6.4 percent in the 2000–2001 academic year to a record total of 547,867, the highest increase since 1980.[18] More than 1.6 million higher education students pursued their studies abroad in 2000, 1.4 million of whom went to developed countries. Half of these students came from developing countries.[19] The total combined foreign expenditures on tuition and living expenses exceeds $12.3 billion worldwide. Over 80 percent of all international undergraduates finance their education in the United States from personal and family sources. In terms of research, 74,571 foreign scholars and scientists were at U.S. academic institutions in 2000, up 5.8 percent over 1998–1999. More than 4 in 10 (43 percent) of foreign scholars in the United States come from Asia. China and India account for 24.3 percent.[20] Constraints of travel, finances, and national barriers restrict international access and argue for international agreements on e-learning, transnational accreditation, and opening of markets to education service providers.

Many people in education and business may be unfamiliar with the set of international agreements that are required for a truly global, transnational education industry. U.S. education providers with industry associations and government agencies have begun to address the issues of international trade barriers in education, largely in response to the World Trade Organization's (WTO) negotiations related to the General Agreement on Trade in Services (GATS). Key U.S. players are The Center for Quality Assurance in International Education, The National Committee for International Trade in Education, and the U.S. Department of Commerce (Service Industries, International Trade Administration). Progress on removing barriers such as national policies on education provision (many states recognize higher education as a product of the state and not of proprietary organizations); intellectual property; telecom laws; limitations on foreign ownership of corporations; and foreign currency regulations are central issues for education companies operating abroad. Agreements and partnerships on e-learning and sales of software and content to locally recognized education institutions find fewer trade barriers, and many U.S. companies are creating markets for these services by pursuing international standards and local accreditation.

From the public data centers in Senegal to the highly wired information cities of Singapore and New York, people experience the world in a way unknown before. Education, knowledge, economic power, and one's sense of identity in a nation, race, and social class have always been mutually reinforcing social forces, but the need to participate in a global economy has produced a broader set of education needs. This reality has been recognized in Europe, where the European Union and globalization drivers are creating new education markets. In March 2001, the Commission of the European Union initiated a new pan-European e-learning plan to be developed by member states and local programs.[21] European leaders are also becoming increasingly aware that education goals can only be achieved by allowing more private and for-profit education providers to enter the marketplace.

BARRIERS AND CHALLENGES TO A GLOBAL E-LEARNING INDUSTRY: INFRASTRUCTURE AND ACCESS ISSUES

Although three in five U.S. households use the Internet and two-thirds of Americans access the Internet from work, North Americans now represent only about 40 percent of global Internet users, and that percentage is shrinking quickly.[22] The top 10 countries with largest concentrations of Internet users are, of course, major e-learning markets with high current levels of education attainment (see Table 4–4).

According to Dataquest, by 2003 the Asia-Pacific region will have more Internet users than North America and

Europe. As Internet access and telecom infrastructure extends through the developing world, more countries are looking to e-learning to provide education for widely dispersed people. Internet connectivity, available regional bandwidth, and local access will remain major infrastructure barriers for worldwide e-learning and Internet-enabled education.

Since the privatization of the Internet in 1994, the U.S. has enjoyed unregulated Internet backbone interconnection, private Internet network peering, and unregulated consumer and retail Internet service provider (ISP) services, a business environment that accounts for the rapid build-out of Internet businesses in the U.S. This is not the case abroad, where infrastructure and access depend on the

TABLE 4–4 Top 10 Countries Using the Internet, by Percentage of Population, 2001

		% ONLINE
1	Sweden	64
2	Iceland	61
3	U.S.	60
4	U.K.	55
5	Hong Kong	54
6	Netherlands	54
7	Norway	54
8	Australia	52
9	Taiwan	52
10	Singapore	49

Source: NUA Internet Surveys, aggregate world survey data.[22]

cooperation of regional and nationalized telecom providers and more recent private entrants. Pricing and access vary greatly, an obstacle for content services like education. The existing trends of international demand for U.S. and European higher education, which has meant large populations of Asian Pacific, Latin American, and African students going to universities in the developed world, will likely be replicated on an even larger scale in online programs. Reaching those markets will, of course, require basic Internet access and partnership with network and telecom systems.

As a result, e-learning business development will inevitably follow the development of the global telecom service infrastructure, summarized in Figure 4.3. One of the greatest challenges ahead will be changing major regional disparities: Some of the regions with the largest populations (i.e., India, China) also have the lowest concentration of telecom infrastructure and computers.

Another way of viewing where the earliest international e-learning markets will grow is through a top-level international network topology map, which shows international bandwidth concentration (see Figure 4.4). The global information economy is a function of high-bandwidth, interconnected, metropolitan areas that form hubs of regional connectivity.[23] U.S.–Europe interconnectivity continues to have the highest capacity, and build-out to other regions

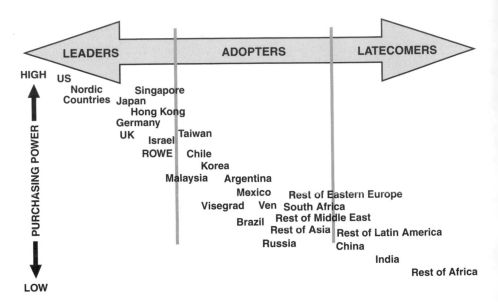

FIGURE 4.3
Worldwide Telecom and Internet Services Distribution. (*Source:* World Bank and Pyramid Research.)

will remain a major challenge of a truly global information economy (see Figure 4.5 and Table 4–5).

International Internet bandwidth grew 174 percent between 2000 and 2001, but many barriers remain (see Table 4–2). Internet usage grows steadily in China, for example, but there are only 8.9 million PCs (0.7 percent penetration) and 124.2 million (10.3 percent penetration) fixed-line phones in China. The cost structure of Internet service to retail customers varies and is generally higher abroad. Unlike most countries, where the cost of Internet access ranges between 1 percent and 5 percent of an individual's monthly income, the cost of Internet access in China is about 10 percent of monthly income.[24]

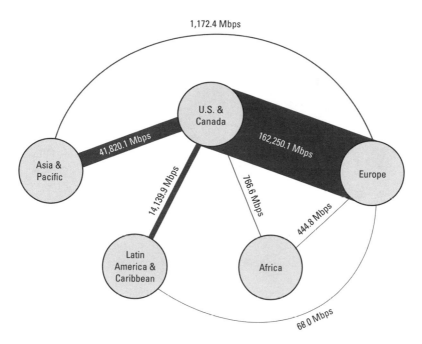

FIGURE 4.4
Major International Internet Routes and Bandwidth. (*Source:* © TeleGeography, Inc. 2001, www.telegeography.com.)

Although strong, the overall rate of growth in international connectivity has slowed from 2001, even though cross-border Internet links increased by 382 percent. The Internet's global topology is growing in uneven spurts. For example, Latin America's international connectivity grew by almost 480 percent to 16.1 gigabits per second (Gbps), largely as a result of new submarine cable systems built by Telefónica and Global Crossing. Although the U.S. still plays a central role in Internet infrastructure, most countries have become less dependent on the U.S. as a switching station. The U.S. remains the world's main hub, however, with

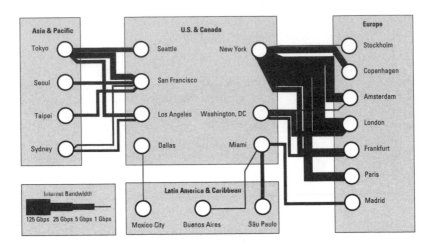

Note: Figure represents Internet bandwidth connected across international borders between Consolidated Metropolitan Statistical Areas or equivalents. Domestic routes are omitted. Data as of mid-2001.

FIGURE 4.5

Major International Internet Routes. (*Source:* © TeleGeography, Inc. 2001, www.telegeography.com.)

over 80 percent of international Internet capacity in Asia, Africa, and South America still connected directly to a U.S. city as of mid-2001.

Industry and government regulatory agreements for international Internet traffic are a major precondition for scalable e-learning across worldwide national boundaries. Telecom policy and international regulation are often seen as a specialized field for lobbyist associations and government relations representatives, and not something that seriously affects business strategy for Internet services. However, for a global e-learning business that depends on expanded worldwide Internet reach and access, this issue requires greater industry partnership and regional involvement.

TABLE 4–5 International Internet Bandwidth by Region, 2000–2001 (by Megabits per Second [Mbps] Capacity)

REGION	2000 MBPS CAPACITY	2001 MBPS CAPACITY	% GROWTH 2000–2001
Africa	649.2	1,230.8	89.6%
Asia	22,965.1	52,661.9	129.3%
Europe	232,316.7	675,637.3	109.8%
Latin America	2,785.2	16,132.5	479.2%
U.S. & Canada	112,222.0	274,184.9	144.3%

Source: TeleGeography, Inc. 2001

CASE STUDIES

We are in a period of remarkable transition and opportunity in worldwide markets, most of which have been more highly regulated and closely linked to a unified national culture and social class system than they are in the U.S. Following the market liberalizing forces in health care, telecom, and IT, the globalized economy is beginning to transform state monopolies in education and credentialing into more open and cooperative public and private systems with common economic goals. This shift in political and economic conditions will open many new opportunities for e-learning companies to enter new markets over the long term.

The following selective case studies illustrate how new business models are emerging to serve worldwide education needs.

UNIVERSITAS 21

Universitas 21 (U21) is an important new model for international university branding and market reach through a global university alliance and a for-profit partnership. At this early stage of international e-learning, U21 provides the most promising model for market reach and acceptance. Thomson Learning is the lead corporate partner for course content and e-learning management. The partnership began as a $50-million joint venture, with U21 and Thomson both committing $25 million as equity partners. Each of the member universities has agreed to invest at least $500,000, and some have pledged as much as $5 million. Profits will be shared among U21, its members, and Thomson. U21 includes two subsidiaries, U21global, the online university, and U21pedagogica, a standards and quality assurance organization. Course offerings will receive multijurisdictional accreditation from the universities that are participating in U21global, but according to Bob Cullen, President and CEO of Thomson Education International, U21global will be self-accredited, based on the quality and acceptance of the member universities' own accreditation.[25]

In late 2001, U21 had 18 member universities in 10 countries, and it will expand to include no more than 25 schools. Its members collectively enroll about 500,000 students, employ some 44,000 academics and researchers, have more than 2 million alumni, and have a combined operating budget of about $9.5 billion. As of fall 2001, New York University and the University of Virginia are the only U.S. institutions participating financially in U21 (see Table 4–6).

The key business strategy is using the U21 alliance brand of leading universities to reach international student markets where demand is high but supply of world-class education is scarce. The first target markets will be Singapore and the Asia-Pacific region followed by Latin America. The Asian-based venture will address the estimated $111-billion global demand for higher education by offering business and technology degrees via U21global, the Internet-based e-learning division, starting in January 2003. The U21global joint venture seeks to offer qualified students on a global basis online, high-quality, internationally portable higher education courses carrying U21 accredita-

TABLE 4–6 Universitas 21 Members

Albert Ludwigs University, Freiburg	University of Glasgow
Fudan University	University of Edinburgh
Lund University	University of Hong Kong
McGill University	University of Melbourne
National University of Singapore	University of New South Wales
Peking University	University of Nottingham
University of Auckland	University of Queensland
University of Birmingham	New York University
University of British Columbia	University of Virginia

tion and certification. U21 will attempt to position itself as the leading international producer and provider of high-quality, professionally relevant education.

U21pedagogica represents an important strategic step for establishing quality assurance for a global education provider. Any international education business operates in an industry with many forms of national accreditation policies and with often jealously guarded professional standards in the control of various national and international academic organizations. Other for-profit higher education companies have met with serious criticism for not providing similar quality and standards processes. U21pedagogica ensures that standards are maintained consistently with relation to admissions; course design, development, pedagogy and courseware; and assessment procedures. This strategy has a dual function: to assure students and the marketplace generally that internationally agreed upon standards for academic program accreditation and course quality are practiced, and to assure faculty and academic professionals that quality will be maintained and that the brands and standards of member universities will not be compromised.

U21 is a very promising model that has been carefully thought out and negotiated. The joint venture allows both partners to focus on core competencies while creating a new value offering that is larger than the sum of its parts. The venture is in its very early stages, but will likely attract imitators for other university and private-sector partnerships.

AFRICAN VIRTUAL UNIVERSITY

Sub-Saharan African nations face many barriers to joining a global knowledge economy, but the World Bank's African Virtual University (AVU) points in the right direction.[26] Only 3 percent of the region's 18- to 25-year-olds enroll in college, and few have any business experience. However, with improved infrastructure and more access to education, Africa will emerge as a large high-demand marketplace for e-learning services. Launched in 1997, AVU now has 26 learning centers in 15 sub-Saharan countries. Students take courses and seminars taught by professors from universities around the world, which are delivered in front of television cameras in the educators' own classrooms. The video is routed via fiber optics, ISDN lines, or satellite to a COMSAT uplink near Washington, DC, which then beams it via satellite to points in Africa. Students are able to talk with the instructors in real time using standard phone lines and Internet chat and email. In addition to courses, AVU offers a digital library with 2,000 full-text journals and a catalog of subject-related Web links.

This is a promising start to distance education in Africa that uses fairly low-cost technology to reach many students. The AVU model is scalable, and with increased economic development through education, African nations will see improvements to infrastructure and access that will enable increased participation in global education.

GLOBAL UNIVERSITY ALLIANCE

The Global University Alliance (GUA; *www.gua.com*), based in Hong Kong, is a partnership of accredited international universities that have joined in a marketing alliance for e-learning programs to expand their global reach, especially in North and South Asia. The participating GUA member institutions are listed in Table 4–7.

They do not have a corporate investor in a joint venture, but they use "portal partners" and their own site to reach online students. The portal companies include Sinohome (*sinohome.com*), China901 (*www.china901.com*), and the South China Morning Post (*www.scmp.com*) for the Chinese market; *ESDlife.com* and *HongKong.com* (for Hong Kong); and English Town (*www.englishtown.com*) for English language skills with a global market. For technology, NextEd, also in Hong Kong, provides the technology infrastructure and system integration for GUA. NextEd partners with Blackboard for the e-learning platform. These international business ventures already represent a sizable new industry with a growing business web of technology service providers and intellectual property companies.

TABLE 4–7 Global University Alliance Members

INSTITUTION	COUNTRY
Athabasca University	Canada
Auckland University of Technology	Australia
George Washington University	U.S.
International Business School	Netherlands
(Hogeschool Brabant)	
The Royal Melbourne Institute of Technology	Australia
The University of Derby	U.K.
University of Glamorgan	U.K.
The University of South Australia	Australia
University of Wisconsin–Milwaukee	U.S.

WORLDWIDE UNIVERSITIES NETWORK

The Worldwide Universities Network (WUN), formed in June 2001, is a graduate-level partnership for the global marketing of members' graduate programs and research. Unlike other international partnerships that focus on undergraduate education and distance learning, the WUN is based primarily on collaboration in research and graduate education. Partner institutions will develop online distributed learning programs for graduate and continuing education.

The founding members in the United States are Pennsylvania State University, University of California–San

Diego, University of Illinois, University of Wisconsin–Madison, and University of Washington. The members from the United Kingdom are the universities of Bristol, Leeds, Manchester, Sheffield, Southampton, and York. The partnership's first programs will be in the areas of bioinformatics, geography of the new economy, public policy and management, smart materials, and nanotechnology.

SYLVAN LEARNING AND SYLVAN INTERNATIONAL UNIVERSITIES

Sylvan has a brand history and market reach that is allowing the company to move quickly into international markets and become a leader in e-learning. The company now has five operating units: Learning Centers, Education Solutions, English Language Instruction, International Universities, and Ventures. In the postsecondary market, Sylvan launched Sylvan International Universities (SIU) in 1999 with a series of acquisitions and ownership stakes in four private, locally accredited institutions: Universidad Europea de Madrid, Les Roches School of Hotel Management, Universidad del Valle de Mexico, and Universidad de Las Americas. Sylvan's current strategy includes localization in foreign markets, blending clicks and bricks for education delivery, following local regulatory environments, and syndicating content across postsecondary units. Sylvan plans to acquire or build new universities in Asia, Latin

America, and southern Europe, areas with market conditions highly favorable to Sylvan's business model. Other postsecondary business units with global reach include the Wall Street Institute (WSI), which provides English language instruction through a combination of computer-based and live instruction. WSI targets the business professional market and now has centers in 23 countries. In online higher education, Sylvan operates four other business units.

Sylvan International uses a two-part strategy: "feet on the ground" local marketing and local regulatory compliance, and building internationally syndicated content and programs for e-learning across national boundaries. The company sees the opportunity clearly and has many competitive advantages in the postsecondary professional and career-based learning market.

AN INTERNATIONAL MANAGEMENT PROGRAM

The International Masters in Practicing Management (IMPM), an attempt to morph the business school into a real-world, international learning context, was founded by Henry Mintzberg, Professor of Management at McGill University in Montreal, Canada, and Jonathan Gosling of Lancaster University Management School, in the U.K. The program consists of modules codeveloped by a consortium of universities "in an authentically international context as a cooperative venture of business schools in five countries around the world—Canada, England, France, India, and Japan. The activities focus on the actual experiences and needs of the participating managers and of their organizations."[28] This innovative program is formed through a consortium of business and management schools: Hitotsubashi University (Tokyo, Japan), Jaist (Ishikawa, Japan), Kobe University (Kobe, Japan), Indian Institute of Management (Bangalore, India), INSEAD (Fontainebleau, France), Lancaster University (Lancaster, England), and McGill University (Montreal, Canada). Instruction and communication are a hybrid of existing methods and contexts, part classroom and part "close learning" through distance-learning study and Internet conferencing. All students must be practiced managers who are sponsored by their companies. There is no "home campus" for IMPM, which consists of two-week modules spread over 16 months and five countries. There are five modules, each one presented by one of the partner universities. Students travel to each campus for one module, spend the time learning the home business culture of each, and then make field study visits to local companies to learn from colleagues there.

The trend of international university consortia developing innovative programs and combining clicks and bricks for local classrooms and online learning will continue. Some universities with international brand names and existing international appeal like the Massachusetts Institute of Technology (MIT) and Duke in the U.S. will expand with satellite campuses and partnerships with universities in other countries. The business of university consortia and international expansion through local campuses and online learning will become a major marketplace for education technology services and content.

These are only a few of many cases in which universities and private-sector companies are developing new business strategies to respond to the worldwide market demand for postsecondary education and e-learning services. This list grows longer weekly. From new business models, new global marketplace inroads, and strategies by education industry leaders, we can extract several critical success factors as the global e-education industry takes off:

- Education offerings must be demand-driven and serve marketplace needs.
- Technology and business model must be scalable.
- Business must exploit the 24/7/365 ubiquitous, on-demand learning environment of the Web.
- Education providers must work toward standardization of credentials and transnational marketplace acceptance.
- There must be dependable infrastructure and user access.

■ Business must find a market entry point with local knowledge and local relationships.

■ Business must find strategic partners to add competencies that solve marketplace problems in ways that you cannot do on your own.

CONCLUDING REFLECTIONS

It is clear that the enormous disparities between education supply and demand provide an unprecedented market opportunity for education services. With this opportunity, however, comes a huge social and economic challenge for developed nations hoping to spread the benefits of globalization to poor countries and expand the global marketplace. Globalization has also created new localizations and reactions against participation in global knowledge. Most people continue to see education as the only hope to forestall impending worldwide catastrophes in cultural misunderstanding and economic disparity. The need to exchange knowledge and learning across borders, cultures, and languages is felt more urgently than ever. This need creates a high profile for the goals of a global e-learning industry, especially when we consider the devastating consequences of ignorance and exclusion from the world marketplace. As Derek Bok, former president of Harvard, is often quoted as saying, "If you think education is expensive, try ignorance."[28]

Many of us who have been involved with the Internet and education for 10 years or more were motivated early on by the great potential to use technology to change education paradigms: to build environments for learner-centered knowledge and information exchange and to provide greater access to knowledge around the world, especially to people who may never see a university campus. These motivations remain, and a new industry is emerging that has the potential to make global access to learning and knowledge a reality. There will be no greater economic force for the long term than education, and the emerging global education industry will be a major world force for many years to come.

ENDNOTES

1. UNESCO, Institute for Statistics, and Merrill Lynch, *The Knowledge Web,* May 2000.

2. "A Global Education Market? Global Business Building Local Markets," Eduventures White Paper, May 2001.

3. UNESCO, Institute for Statistics, and Merrill Lynch, *The Knowledge Web*, May 2000.

4. The idea of a business web was described by Don Tapscott, David Ticoll, and Alex Lowy in *Digital Capital: Harnessing the Power of Business Webs* (Boston: Harvard Business School Press, 2000).

5. UNESCO, Institute for Statistics, *Facts and Figures 2000.*

6. World Bank data, 2001.

7. See James Tooley, "The Global Education Industry: Lessons from Private Education in Developing Countries." Online data and publications available at *www.ifc.org/publications/* and *www.worldbank.org/edinvest/*.

8. UNESCO Press, *www.unesco.org/opi/eng/unescopress/2001/01-99e.shtml.* Other key worldwide education indicators and statistics can be found at the UNESCO Institute for Statistics, *http://unescostat.unesco.org/*.

9. See James Tooley, *The Global Education Industry* (London: Institute for Economic Analysis, 1999) and *UNESCO Courier*, November 2000.

10. Cited in Peter Stokes' "A Global Education Market? Global Business Building Local Markets," Eduventures White Paper, May 2001.

11. The report with downloadable tables can be found at *www.unesco.org/education/information/wer/index.htm.*

12. Quoted in *Financial Times*, January 5, 2001.

13. The report with downloadable tables can be found at *www.unesco.org/education/information/wer/index.htm.*

14. Detailed data on language use and issues for multilingual domain name administration can be found in the documents for WIPO's meeting on multilingual domain names at *www.itu.int/mdns/briefingpaper/index.html.*

15. NUA Internet Surveys and IDG.net, October 8, 2001; see *www.nua.ie/surveys/.*

16. *www.glreach.com/globstats/.* References to data sources and methodology are found on the site.

17. Source: Institute of International Education, online: at *www.iienetwork.org.*

18. UNESCO, Institute for Statistics, *Facts and Figures 2000*, and the National Committee for International Trade in Education (*www.tradeineducation.org*).

19. Data from the Institute of International Education's Open Doors, *www.opendoorsweb.org.*

20. See the EU's e-learning site with references to the Council's actions at *europa.eu.int/comm/education/elearning/index.html*, and the Eurydice Information Network on Education in Europe at *www.eurydice.org.*

21. Gartner Dataquest, September 3, 2001; NUA Internet Surveys and Xylo, August 24, 2001; NUA Internet Surveys and NielsenNetRatings, August 31, 2001.

22. NUA Internet Surveys, "How Many Online," composite totals from current worldwide data sources: *www.nua.com/surveys/how_many_online/index.html*.

23. Telegeography, *Packet Geography 2002*, online at *www.telegeography.com/products/books/pg/index.html*.

24. See Asia & Pacific Internet Association, *Newsletter 7, Country Profile: China*, online at *www.apia.org/pdf/newsletter7.pdf*.

25. Information on U21 and U21global is from company information and a conversation with Bob Cullen, October 29, 2001.

26. See AVU Web site at *www.avu.org/*. Other coverage of e-education in Africa includes: Osei Darkwa and Fikile Mazibuko, "Creating Virtual Learning Communities in Africa: Challenges and Prospects," *First Monday 5.5*, online at *www.firstmonday.dk/issues/issue5_5/darkwa/index.html*; David A. Light, "Pioneering Distance Education in Africa," *Harvard Business Review*, September–October 1999; and the World Bank's Knowledgebank information at *www.worldbank.org/knowledgebank/facts/avu.html*.

27. From Web site *www.impm.org/overfrm.htm*. See article on Mintzberg and IMPM in *Fast Company, 40*, online at *www.fastcompany.com/online/40/wf_mintzberg.html*.

28. Bok, Derek, *Universities and the Future of America.* Chapel Hill, NC, Duke University Press, 1990, p. 105.

5

QUALITY, COST AND ACCESS: THE CASE FOR REDESIGN

—Carol A. Twigg

CENTER FOR ACADEMIC TRANSFORMATION, RENSSELAER POLYTECHNIC INSTITUTE

Few organizational systems within American society consider the norms and practices that have evolved over the years as much a truism as education. The bell rings at 3 P.M. Students are organized by age group. Elementary education is taught by generalists, whereas junior high school and high school education are taught by subject specialists. Applications to college are painstakingly typed. The list goes on. Stepping onto a college campus in 2002—as the information economy gains speed—a visitor from 1950 would be right at home. Professors lecture. Teaching assistants manage course sections. Few courses draw from interdisciplinary faculties. Students sit in rows facing the blackboard. The quad is at the center of campus life.

No consideration of the impact of e-learning on higher education would be complete without considering how Internet technologies are, or are not, changing the "traditional" structure of a college course. Are we grafting the age-old way of teaching Biology 101 onto the Internet, or are we using the native capabilities of technology to change Biology 101 for the better? The question has been tackled by Carol Twigg, for many years now, most recently in her capacity as Director of the Center for Academic Transformation. Through her work funding and reviewing course redesigns across institutions and disciplines, Dr. Twigg has a front-row seat to the potential and likelihood of e-learning creating change in the teaching and learning environment on campus and beyond.

In this chapter, Twigg guides the reader through a bottoms-up consideration of how courses are organized, the strengths and weaknesses of the traditional model, the potential of Internet technologies, and the measurable impact course redesigns through technology have had already at institutions participating in her Center's programs. Unlike the top-down views of Levine, Cappelli, and Irvine in the preceding chapters, Twigg in this chapter and Don Spicer in Chapter 6, "Where the Rubber Meets the Road: An On-Campus Perspective of a CIO," respec-

tively, shift our thinking from trends to tactics. At the end of the day, the degree to which e-learning influences the relationship between faculty member and student is the crux of its impact. Twigg's work "in the trenches" offers one of the best opportunities to roll up our sleeves and see for ourselves.

Carol A. Twigg is Executive Director of the Center for Academic Transformation at Rensselaer Polytechnic Institute, the mission of which is to serve as a source of expertise and support for those in higher education who wish to take advantage of the capabilities of information technology (IT) to transform their academic practices. The Center manages The Pew Learning and Technology Program, a $8.8-million, four-year effort sponsored by the Pew Charitable Trusts to place the national discussion about the impact of IT on campus in the context of student learning and ways to achieve this learning cost-effectively. The Center also conducts The Leadership Forum, a series of activities designed to advance the growth of knowledgeable people to lead their institutions, companies, and organizations in the Information Age.

From 1993 through 1998, Twigg served as Vice President of Educom, a nonprofit consortium of 600 colleges and universities dedicated to the transformation of higher education through the application of IT. Before joining Educom, she served as Associate Vice Chancellor for Learning Technologies for the State University of New York

(SUNY). For 16 years prior to that, she held a number of senior academic administrative positions at SUNY Empire State College. She has taught at SUNY/Buffalo, the State University College at Buffalo, and Empire State College. She received her BA from the College of William and Mary and a PhD in English Literature from SUNY/Buffalo. Newsweek named her as one of the 50 most influential thinkers in the Information Revolution.

How significant will the impact of the Internet be on higher education? Put simply, I believe the Internet will enable the transformation of education at all levels. This does not mean that all who are currently involved in higher education will necessarily participate in that transformation. Some will simply not want to; they lack the desire. Others will not devote the necessary resources; they lack the will. Some will not have the necessary skills; they lack the commitment to either develop them or partner with others who are able to bring such skills to their institution.

Transformation is hard work; it takes a lot of time and effort. It's not something that magically happens by deciding "we will be transformed simply by virtue of technology's existence." I believe the faculty and staff that are seriously involved in the activities and programs at the Center for Academic Transformation (*www.center.rpi.edu/*), which I direct, are truly transforming higher education. Today most of the nation's faculty who are using technology are simply putting their courses online. Our faculty project leaders are doing much more; they are fundamentally redesigning the way courses are developed and delivered.

The Center for Academic Transformation's mission is to serve as a source of expertise and support for those in higher education who wish to take advantage of the capabilities of IT to transform their academic practices. The Center manages a $6-million program called the Pew Grant Program in Course Redesign (*www.center.rpi.edu/PewGrant.html*), a four-year effort sponsored by the Pew Charitable Trusts.

What we are beginning to accomplish at the Center is the establishment of a whole new way of thinking about higher education, a new way of thinking about how to use IT in the academic program, and a new way of thinking about course design. The faculty and staff involved in these efforts are first to market with these new ideas. They are pointing the way to future developments in the use of technology in the academic program. Our interest in using IT is to find ways in which we can address higher education's major challenges: the familiar mantra of improving quality, increasing access, and reducing cost.

Today, the world of e-learning is doing a lot to tackle the access problem. We still have a long way to go, but there's a growing availability of online courses that reach out to students in ways that have never been possible before.

However, when we look at the dimensions of quality and cost, we are just beginning.

At the crux of the quality issue in distance and e-learning is the no-significant-difference phenomenon. Much of the discussion that occurs on campus consists of technology advocates trying to prove that online courses are as good as traditional education. Instead, we should be thinking about how to make online courses even better than traditional courses.

Many people on campus are searching for evidence that investing in technology can save money in the long run by addressing the underlying economics of educational delivery. At this point, technology seems to be addressing the issue of costs by driving them up! We are a long way from truly thinking about using technology to control or reduce costs. In my view, we need to help institutions understand how investments in technology can, in fact, generate a return on that investment.

To use technology to deal with both major issues simultaneously—cost and quality—you must first examine several assumptions about the relationships among quality, cost, and IT. These assumptions dominate the current discussion, making it difficult to find creative solutions. The first assumption most people in higher education make is that improving quality means adding resources and increasing cost. Higher quality means a bigger budget: more full-time faculty, bigger libraries, bigger laboratories, and bigger networks. Conversely, controlling costs means reducing quality (e.g., relying on large lecture courses); increasing the use of adjuncts, teaching assistants (TAs), and other part-time faculty; or, most drastically, laying off faculty. Very few people in higher education believe that it is possible to increase quality and reduce costs at the same time. A second assumption is that adding IT to the mix only increases higher education's cost. Very few believe that investments in IT can generate a return on that investment, not only in terms of increased quality but also in reduced costs.

Why do people think this way? It comes down to a pretty simple proposition: If we think about the two predominant forms of instruction on our campuses today, they remain the stand-up lecture, which I assure you is alive and well in higher education, and the smaller, more interactive seminar, or small-class model. To date, when we have applied technology to higher education, we have simply bolted technology onto our existing formats.

Although the televised lecturer is still popular in many states, the current infatuation is with the online small seminar. Advocates of the latter model argue that you cannot possibly have more than 15 students in an online class. As mentioned earlier, a clear consequence of this approach is that by replicating familiar pedagogical modes, the courses will simply be as good as regular classroom instruction. Ideally, people should think about redesigning their pedagogical processes rather than simply layering technology onto what they have always done. In short, they need to examine some of the basic premises of instruction.

To address these issues, the Center's programs encourage colleges and universities to redesign their approaches to instruction using technology to achieve both cost savings and quality enhancements. In other words, we're trying to show institutions that they can, in fact, have their cake and eat it, too.

At the Center we are trying to change the world, but we are not trying to change it all at one time. We are focusing on a particular set of courses: large-enrollment introductory courses. The reasons for doing so are compelling. Maricopa Community College in Arizona enrolls more than 100,000 students in any given year. In an internal study, Maricopa found that it offers 2,000 individual courses, not sections, but distinctly titled, stand-alone courses. Maricopa's study also found that 25 of those courses account for 44 percent of their total enrollment. In other words, the other 1,975 courses make up 56 percent—so 44 percent of their enrollment is concentrated in just those 25 courses. Other community colleges have conducted similar studies, and their numbers are more typically 51 percent or 52 percent in those 25 courses. At the baccalaureate level, these same courses account for approximately 35 percent of total enrollment.

The insight these figures provide is simple and compelling: If you want to have a considerable impact on large numbers of students, you should focus on the 25 courses where most students are actually enrolled, as opposed to putting disparate kinds of courses online, spending a lot of energy impacting a relatively small number of people. The higher enrollment courses are, as one would expect, introductory courses in math, science, English, and the social sciences. This high-impact list is the target group for the Center's redesigns.

In addition to having an impact on large numbers of students, there are other advantages of such a focus. First, large introductory courses are good prospects for technology-enhanced redesign because they have a more or less standardized curriculum, outcomes that can be easily delineated, and content over which faculty are less possessive. In other words, there is not a lot of argument about what a course like college algebra should include. There may be some dispute around the edges, but compared to advanced-level courses in which there are raging theoretical debates, introductory courses benefit from a high level of agreement. Faculty are relatively less possessive of these courses and more inclined to work collaboratively to establish common goals and common objectives. This is a critical characteristic because course redesigns begin by identifying the student learning outcomes that the faculty are trying to achieve and then figuring out alternative routes to get there.

We know, too, that introductory courses are a prime area of ineffective teaching. We know that failure rates are quite high in these courses. The transition from freshman year to sophomore year is the moment when campuses see a spike in the number of dropouts. If we can address the underlying problems in the design of these introductory courses, we can go a long way toward increasing retention in our institutions. Furthermore, introductory courses have a big influence on future majors. Everyone knows students who say, "I want to be a chemistry major," only to watch them take their first introductory chemistry course in college and then quickly switch to psychology. If we can make improvements in these introductory courses and give students a good foundation, the likelihood of their staying with some of the more difficult subjects is greater.

In addition, these courses serve as feeders to other disciplines, so other faculty and departments depend heavily on what goes on in them. What too frequently happens is that students do not learn the introductory material very well. The follow-on faculty then begin beating up on the introductory-level faculty, saying, "What's wrong with you people? Why aren't you teaching these students?" The impact on other disciplines is thus equally important.

Finally, our project has gathered a lot of data about what introductory courses generally cost, and we know they consume a significant amount of institutional resources. Despite the common wisdom that packed lecture halls and low-paid graduate teaching assistants equal the most cost-effective way to deal with large numbers of students, lecture-based courses are not cheap. In many institutions, introductory courses are taught in multiple sections by individual faculty members, quite costly given the large number of sections required. For example, at the University of Wisconsin at Madison, approximately $1 million per year is spent teaching introductory chemistry. If institutions can effectively redesign these introductory courses, it will free up more resources—a double advantage.

The Center has awarded grants of $200,000 to 30 institutions to redesign large-enrollment introductory courses under the auspices of the Pew Grant Program in Course Redesign. We have funded a fairly wide range of curriculum projects at a diverse group of institutions. These include redesign efforts in chemistry at the University of Wisconsin at Madison, statistics at Penn State, linear algebra at Virginia Tech, and Spanish at the University of Tennessee. At Riverside Community College, we are supporting a redesign of college algebra and at the State University of New York at Buffalo we are funding a redesign in computer literacy. We have also funded redesigns of humanities courses in such areas as fine arts, world civilization, and English composition.

Beyond focusing on key points of leverage within an institution, we need to look at how most introductory courses are taught. In short, we must take aim at the tried and true lecture. Frankly, when people talk about wiring podiums, it makes my hair stand on end because the lecture-based approach to instruction suffers from so many problems (see

Figure 5.1). First, the lecture is a push technology. It treats students as if they were all the same, as if they come to the course with the same levels of ability, the same levels of interest, and the same goals for completing the course. It is very difficult to respond individually to students in the lecture format.

Furthermore, the lecture is a one-way technology. We know that it is very ineffective in engaging students. Once a class size gets larger than 30 to 35 students, it might as well be 300 or 3,000 because the ability to actively engage

FIGURE 5.1
What's Wrong with the Lecture?

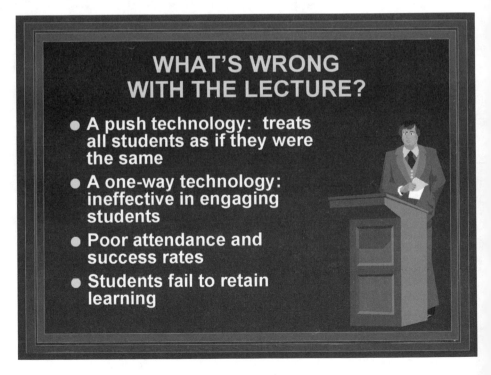

students just about disappears. We know, too, that lecture courses suffer from poor attendance and poor success rates. We also know that students fail to retain the learning that they acquire in lectures. In other words, they might get passing grades, but when it comes to applying that learning, the perils of cramming at the last minute and passing exams really become clear.

Using multiple sections, which is the other way in which introductory courses are taught, presents a number of problems as well (see Figure 5.2). When courses are taught in multiple sections, they often suffer from a lack of coordination and consistency because faculty members tend to do their own thing, whether they're adjuncts or full-time faculty. A second problem in using multiple sections is that course development is typically done individually. You find faculty standing in room after room, all doing essentially the same thing, which is very labor-intensive. Nothing is being shared. When a professor does something particularly well, there is no easy way to transfer that success to other faculty members teaching the same course, other than anecdotally. The multiple-section model also produces inconsistent learning outcomes. There is little correlation between student abilities when they come in and the learning results at the end of the process, because there is such variation among the sections. If multiple sections are being created individually, it is difficult for faculty members to learn from one another and incorporate materials into the

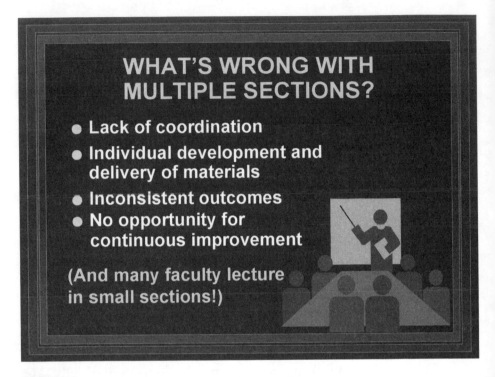

FIGURE 5.2
What's Wrong with Multiple Sections?

course. Most important, there is no opportunity for continuous improvement.

Furthermore, even in small sections many faculty continue to lecture. I well remember an English course I took
at William and Mary during my senior year, a Victorian literature seminar with a class of nine. Three times a week,
the professor lectured beautifully because this was the way
he had been taught to teach; his Harvard training served
him well. It did not matter that there were only nine

students in the room. All too frequently, this goes on in small classes across the country.

All of our redesign projects are employing a number of similar pedagogical techniques. The key to these redesigns is to break what has been called the credit-for-contact model. In other words, rather than assuming that all students need to be in a classroom for 45 hours, no matter what the subject matter or what their preparation, the course redesigners ask, "When do students really need to be in class? When do they not need to be in class? Why do they need to be in class? What other kinds of more meaningful learning activities can substitute for simply going to class?"

All of the Center-supported redesigns emphasize active learning rather than passive note taking. They call for greater student engagement with the materials. As one math professor is fond of saying, "Students learn math not by watching somebody doing math on the board, but by actively being engaged in doing math and solving problems." They move away from the concept of the faculty member talking and presenting materials toward creating opportunities for active student engagement.

Almost all the projects use some form of self-paced interactive materials, which are frequently the cornerstone of these redesigns (see Figure 5.3). Rather than relying on a single faculty member leading chat rooms or sending

SELF-PACED INTERACTIVE MATERIALS

- Interactive tutorials and exercises = needed student practice
- Computerized, low-stakes quizzes = feedback, repetition and reinforcement
- Teach abstract concepts interactively
  - Greater hands-on experience with data analysis/collection
  - Illustrate concepts visually
- Examples from various disciplines
- Respond to differences in learning style
- Opportunities to refresh knowledge

FIGURE 5.3
Self-Paced Interactive Materials.

emails, these designs take advantage of computer-based learning materials such as self-paced interactive tutorials and exercises. Students thus have a greater opportunity to practice by reviewing a concept if they fail to learn it the first time. Computerized low-stakes quizzes allow greater feedback, more repetition, and reinforcement of what the students know and do not know. Too often today, faculty reach the midterm exam only to discover that a large number of the students have not learned the material. As a result, a major aspect of our new designs is the correction of weaknesses early in the course.

Once you break away from the push technology of the lecture, you are able to respond to students who have needs in particular areas rather than treating them all the same. In each of these redesigns, we offer more individualized assistance to students. In addition, these designs emphasize collaboration and the creation of learning teams. When they think about technology-enhanced courses, many people have an image of students sitting in front of terminals typing or perhaps being mesmerized. However, the Center's redesigns typically create opportunities for group work, group projects, and some very elaborate learning team strategies. They all promote 24/7 access to learning resources and are increasingly promoting the notion that those resources stay available to students when they move on to subsequent courses (see Figure 5.4).

New kinds of computer-based materials allow faculty to teach abstract concepts much more interactively, allowing statistics courses, for example, to emphasize hands-on experience with data analysis and collection. Again the goal is for students to be doing statistics, rather than hearing about how to do statistics. The materials are able to illustrate concepts visually, an approach that is particularly effective in such sciences as biology and astronomy. Rather than listening to someone lecture about scientific concepts,

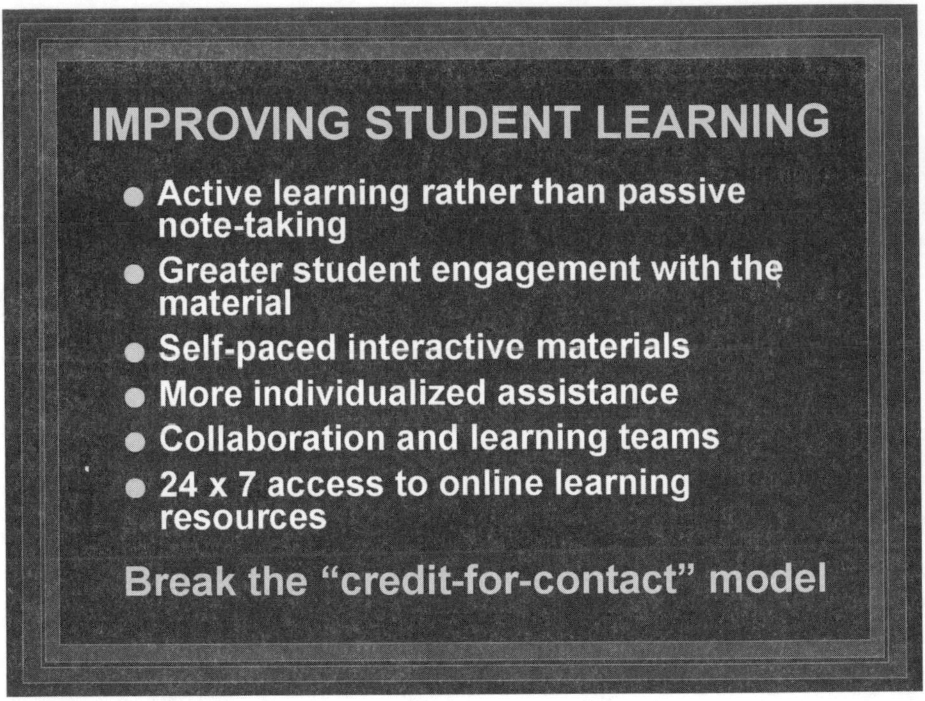

IMPROVING STUDENT LEARNING

- Active learning rather than passive note-taking
- Greater student engagement with the material
- Self-paced interactive materials
- More individualized assistance
- Collaboration and learning teams
- 24 x 7 access to online learning resources

Break the "credit-for-contact" model

FIGURE 5.4
Improving Student Learning.

students have the opportunity to interact with and manipulate visual illustrations. Another advantage of relying on Web-based learning materials is that educators can use examples from multiple disciplines within the same course. In a math course, for example, you can have examples from business, nursing, engineering, and agriculture, multiple examples that respond more effectively to individual students' interests.

All of the course redesigns attempt to respond to differences in student learning preferences. Florida Gulf Coast

University, one of the newest institutions in Florida, has a required general education course for all freshmen during which they analyze their learning styles as preparation for future work within the university. The institution uses the data to construct various types of learning activities and, in turn, assesses how successful different approaches are with different kinds of students.

How about reducing costs? Just as there are a variety of approaches to improving the quality of student learning, so too are there a variety of approaches to reducing instructional costs. There is not just one simple answer. What characterizes these 30 course redesigns is a range of instructional models that vary according to a particular institutional situation. At the same time, what the Center has discovered is that there are three fundamental approaches to cost reduction.

First, an institution might seek to maintain constant enrollment while reducing the amount of resources devoted to the course. The key to this approach is reducing the amount of resources while carrying the same number of students and increasing their learning ability. Second, if an institution is in growth mode, it might seek to increase enrollments while maintaining the same level of resources. For example, the University of Illinois at Urbana-Champaign has a tremendous demand for Spanish, which it was unable to meet because it could not hire enough Spanish professors—full-time or adjuncts. Using new techniques, the university has been able to double the number of students in its redesigned Spanish sections and has effectively opened the bottleneck in Spanish.

A third approach to reducing costs is reducing course repetitions. At many community colleges, for example, it takes a student about two and a half times to pass introductory math courses. Clearly, if you can move students through in a more expeditious fashion by having them pass in one and a half times—we're not looking for perfection—you will generate tremendous savings in resources, both at the institutional level and for the students. At one prominent community college, it takes 37,000 student enrollments to produce 800 students who have successfully completed their math requirements—an incredibly small throughput for these key introductory courses. Not surprisingly, the Center has found that a lot of the redesign projects are trying two of these approaches simultaneously. All of the projects are trying to reduce attrition, while either trying to increase enrollment or reduce the amount of resources devoted to the course.

How does the Center go about helping institutions think about strategies for cost reduction? We have developed a spreadsheet-based course planning tool (see *www.center. rpi.edu/PewGrant/Tool.html*) to assist them in conducting an instructional task analysis on which financial planning can be based. University and college faculty fill out the planning tool, which sounds somewhat miraculous, but some of them actually enjoy it! The first task we ask them to do is calculate all the personnel costs associated with offering the course. Remember, what we are doing is redesigning full courses, not individual classes. If you look at a full introductory course, you typically find many different kinds of personnel participating. You may have TAs, undergraduate peer tutors, professional staff, and adjunct faculty in addition to full-time faculty. The spreadsheet is used to calculate an hourly rate for all of the people who contribute to the course.

We then ask the faculty to determine the specific tasks associated with offering a course and how much time each person spends on each of the various tasks. Next, we calculate the total instructional costs for the traditional method of offering the course for both preparation and delivery (see Figures 5.5 and 5.6). We are breaking down all of the aspects of teaching a course into discrete tasks. Finally, the faculty use the same process to analyze the course redesign and to recalculate the costs (see Figures 5.7 and 5.8). The tool then translates the data to a total cost per student. Based on the number of students in the course, you can extrapolate that number out to the full cost of offering the course.

Why is this specific task analysis so important? When faculty begin to see how much time they are spending, for example, on test preparation, they are motivated to seek alternatives. If you look at each of the elements involved in

Traditional Course Preparation

	FACULTY		TAs/GAs	
	Hourly rate =	$132	Hourly rate =	$23
I. Course Preparation	# of Hours	Total Cost	# of Hours	Total Cost
A. Curriculum Development				
B. Materials Acquistion				
C. Materials Development				
1. Lectures/presentations	60	$7,900	464	$10,510
2. Learning materials/software				
3. Diagnostic assessments				
4. Assignments				
5. Tests/evaluations	12	$1,580	88	$1,993
Sub-Total	72	$9,480	552	$12,503
D. Faculty/TA Devmt/Training				
1. Orientation			240	$5,436
2. Staff meetings	15	$1,975	120	$2,718
3. Attend lectures			240	$5,436
Sub-Total	15	$1,975	600	$13,590
Total Preparation	87	$11,455	1152	$26,093

FIGURE 5.5
Traditional Course Preparation Cost Worksheet.

course design and delivery, you recognize that companies are beginning to emerge that supply either the materials or services for each one. If there is a good test available as part of the textbook from a publisher, for example, the instructor gains access to high-quality assessment materials that have been tested over large populations and can eliminate the work of the test preparation, which is a tremendous advantage.

Our projects are investigating the whole process of course design and delivery and trying to decide, for exam-

Traditional Course Delivery

II. Course Delivery	# of Hours	Total Cost	# of Hours	Total Cost
A. Instruction				
1. Diagnose skill/knowledge level				
2. Presentation	30	$3,950		
3. Interaction	30	$3,950	1048	$23,737
4. Progress monitoring				
Sub-Total	60	$7,900	1048	$23,737
B. Evaluation				
1. Test proctoring	11	$1,448	32	$725
2. Tests/evaluation	12	$1,580	648	$14,677
Sub-Total	23	$3,028	680	$15,402
Total Delivery	83	$10,929	1728	$39,139
TOTAL	170	$22,384	2880	$65,232
Support Staff = $3805				
GRAND TOTAL	$91,421			
Total # of students	350			
Cost per student	$261.20			

FIGURE 5.6
Traditional Course Delivery Cost Worksheet.

ple, where faculty really need to interact with students and where they would be better served by utilizing other kinds of approaches. Using this method, they literally examine every single aspect of the process and make different decisions depending on their circumstances, the kinds of students they are serving, and the subject matter they are teaching.

Let's consider two examples—one is a large lecture course and the other a multiple-section course—that show how worthwhile the effort of doing this analysis and

Redesigned Course Preparation

I. Course Preparation	FACULTY		TAs/GAs	
	# of Hours	Total Cost	# of Hours	Total Cost
A. Curriculum Development	Hourly rate =	$132	Hourly rate =	$23
B. Materials Acquistion				
C. Materials Development				
1. Lectures/presentations	15	$1,975	224	$5,074
2. Learning materials/software				
3. Diagnostic assessments				
4. Assignments				
5. Tests/evaluations	12	$1,580	88	$1,993
Sub-Total	27	$3,555	312	$7,067
D. Faculty/TA Devmt/Training				
1. Orientation			240	$5,436
2. Staff meetings	15	$1,975	120	$2,718
3. Attend lectures			120	$2,718
Sub-Total	15	$1,975	480	$10,872
Total Preparation	42	$5,530	792	$17,939

FIGURE 5.7
Redesigned Course Preparation Cost Worksheet.

redesign can be. The first example is a general chemistry course, a typical lecture–lab–recitation model that we find in many institutions. One of the academic problems that the chemistry faculty have identified is that students enter the course with inconsistent academic preparation. This example happens to be at a prestigious institution where the students are well qualified and well prepared. However, in a subject like chemistry, some students may have loved it in high school, whereas others hated it; thus, they bring very different attitudes to the course. Students are taking

Redesigned Course Delivery

II. Course Delivery	# of Hours	Total Cost	# of Hours	Total Cost
A. Instruction				
1. Diagnose skill/knowledge				
2. Presentation	30	$3,950		
3. Interaction	30	$3,950	808	$18,301
4. Progress monitoring				
Sub-Total	60	$7,900	808	$18,301
B. Evaluation				
1. Test proctoring	11	$1,448	32	$725
2. Tests/evaluation	12	$1,580	408	$9,241
Sub-Total	23	$3,028	440	$9,966
Total Delivery	83	$10,929	1248	$28,267
TOTAL	125	$16,459	2040	$46,206
Support Staff Carryover		$3,805		
Additional Support Staff	480	$3,360		
Total Support Staff		$7,165		
GRAND TOTAL		$69,830		
Total # of students	350			
Cost per student	$199.51			

FIGURE 5.8
Redesigned Course Delivery Cost Worksheet.

the course for various reasons to meet a range of requirements, and so there are many different levels of motivation. Faculty at this university also understand that the lecture method cannot accommodate individual learning styles, and they are concerned that students have inadequate interaction with the materials.

Faculty are also concerned about failure and D grade rates in the course. At this particular institution the D grade, fail, withdraw (D/F/W) rate is about 15 percent, a statistic the Center is discovering holds pretty constant across large research institutions for introductory courses. At comprehensive universities and state colleges, the D/F/W rate tends to be 30 percent to 40 percent. In community colleges, it can run as high as 50 percent to 60 percent in these introductory courses. In the case of this institution, what is more important than the D/F/W rate is the students' inability to retain what they learn, something Professor Lee Schulman has called *amnesia*. Students will say, "I know I learned it, I just can't remember it." Similarly, students are unable to apply foundation principles to other disciplines, what Schulman has called *inertia*. Students say, "I think I knew how to do it, but I somehow forgot as I made the transition to the next discipline."[1]

What are the academic goals for the redesigned course? In sum, faculty members want to address all of the academic problems they have identified. They want to enhance quality by providing greater individualization of instruction. They want to assess students' knowledge in much smaller subject-matter chunks with the goal of providing feedback and direction so that students can begin to make up for their own deficiencies. Rather than the professor correcting every little problem, students begin to learn how to do it themselves by interacting with the materials and self-testing. The faculty team wants to incorporate examples and information from other disciplines and provide a means by which these course materials can be reviewed in subsequent courses.

This chemistry redesign is very conservative; it is not a radical revolution. The faculty plan to eliminate one lecture and keep another lecture, eliminate one discussion section and keep a second one, and leave the labs basically unchanged. They will add a help lab where students can access both interactive learning modules and tutorial assistance. (Students can interact with the materials at other times as well.) By the time the result of all these changes is calculated, the savings are about $300,000 a year. The cost of an individual section drops to about $65,000 versus the $90,000 it cost to offer it in the traditional format. Multiply this cost by the total number of sections offered each year and the savings becomes $300,000 in real dollars that will accumulate year after year. These surplus resources can be reinvested in other courses, used to buy technology, or redistributed in whatever way the faculty and institution choose. I want to emphasize again that this is a very modest redesign.

To give an example of course redesign involving multiple sections, I'll use a linear algebra course. The academic problems the course faces are pretty similar to what goes on in the large lecture example. Although offered in 38 small sections, the course suffers from inconsistent student academic preparation, inability to accommodate different learning styles, retention problems, and the amnesia and inertia problems mentioned before. In addition, the lack of uniformity in learning outcomes is a key problem in this multiple-section course. There is no way that the institution can assure that students have similar high-quality learning experiences when they take different sections of the course. The academic goals for the redesign are also very similar to the large lecture example: individualized instruction, more frequent assessment, a just-in-time response system that is available 75 to 80 hours a week, and the ability to incorporate examples and information from other disciplines into the course materials.

A key feature of the redesigned format is the faculty's ability to make changes in the course as it proceeds, so that continuous improvement becomes a built-in feature. This means that if students get to a particular type of math problem that they become stuck on, the faculty immediately know that there is a problem with the way they developed the material and can pull it out. The problem can be corrected, put back in, retested, and reabsorbed into the materials. Each year the course can be continuously improved, with new features added to an existing body of material, something that is not possible when individual faculty members do their own thing.

In the traditional format, the course was taught in 38 sections. Because of the variety of instructional personnel that participated—10 tenured faculty members, 13 adjunct instructors, and 15 graduate TAs—there was tremendous variability. In the redesign they created one 1,500-student section.

In other words, the concept of multiple sections is completely gone. There is simply one section that takes place in a 24/7 computer laboratory. One tenured faculty member and one instructor manage the course, and a series of graduate and undergraduate helpers provide individualized assistance to students. Because this course is run off large databases, adding two technical staff was required. The result is that the university has gone from a per-student cost of approximately $77 to $24—a two-thirds reduction.

The linear algebra course employed a far more radical redesign than the chemistry course, but both examples illustrate how similar techniques will produce similar successful results. Overall, courses in our project average a savings of about 40 percent, and collectively the 30 courses involved represent a savings of about $3.6 million annually.

What are some of the labor-saving techniques that these projects are using? The key idea is that the students are doing the work, not the faculty. If you walk past a traditional classroom, the faculty member is standing in the front, waving his or her hands, presenting his or her slides or writing on the board, while the students sit quietly taking notes. In these new classrooms, when you walk past and look in, the students are doing all the work. They are waving their hands. They are showing their fellow students examples of projects. The faculty member is sitting back and observing, responding to students when necessary, because his or her primary energy has gone into the design.

All of these redesigns reduce the number of lectures or class meetings. Some throw them out completely. Others may retain one or two of them. There is a lot of variability—there is no one right answer—because it all depends on the nature of the subject matter and the student audience. All of the course redesigns reduce the amount of presentation time. This does not mean that the faculty never give a presentation. Typically, they might give a 15-minute overview to introduce the subject, but then engage students in much more active learning exercises.

Within these course redesigns, all faculty use some kind of course management software to monitor student performance. The student may call up at the end of the semester and ask, "Why am I getting a D?" The faculty member is able to say, "Well, perhaps it's because you've only spent 10 hours on the materials in the entire semester." They know exactly whether or not students have been engaged in learning.

Many of the redesigns have automated the grading of homework, quizzes, and exams. They vary from highly sophisticated projects to less sophisticated approaches. Carnegie Mellon University uses an intelligent tutoring system as part of their statistics course, and the University of Illinois at Urbana-Champaign uses Mallard, software that automates the grading of grammatical exercises in foreign languages and applied problems in economics. Again, we are trying to generate a range of approaches to serve as examples of what can be achieved.

You will also find that all faculty save on class time by moving illustrations and assessments to the Web. Class time is simply wasted by standing up and presenting materials that students could easily access online. Many of our projects are using online materials to train TAs or adjuncts, thus enabling more consistent quality control when multiple personnel are involved. Most of the redesigns rely on replacing one-on-one interaction and the 100 to 200 email phenomenon with greater emphasis on peer-to-peer interaction and other strategies.

Some design strategies substitute less expensive, less expert labor for expensive faculty time where it is appropriate. Rio Salado College, for example, has quadrupled the number of students in its introductory mathematics courses by adding a course assistant position. Rio found that 90 percent of the questions that faculty members were getting had absolutely nothing to do with the academic substance of the course. The questions tended to be things like "When's the test?" or "When is the paper due?" Allowing the assistant to respond to these types of questions permits the faculty member to concentrate on the important academic interactions with students and the course design.

What do the faculty say about the course redesigns? Most say that it is the best experience they have ever had in a classroom. Faculty members themselves are tired of doing the same thing year after year. Most of those who are engaged in various kinds of online learning projects experience a rejuvenating effect, even though they sometimes complain about how much initial work is involved. However, the work is very exciting and very stimulating. I believe part of the success of these projects is the fact that faculty are working collaboratively on the total course design. Through joint planning, they are learning a lot from their peers and the experiences that go beyond simply working with technology. In line with this, the faculty are saying that the quality of their work life has changed immeasurably for the better. They all say that there is a lot of work during the transition, but it is truly worth the effort. They know that the end result will be a "product" that they can continue to work on and improve as they move throughout their careers.

Returning to my opening statement on the transformative potential of the Internet in higher education, for me the proof lies in the simple, yet powerful redesigns described in this chapter. The end result of our project will likely be more than 30 different models at diverse institutions, with different kinds of students and in different kinds of disciplines. These models will share many things in common, both the pedagogical techniques and cost-saving techniques that I've mentioned, but each will have its own unique twist. What is significant is that these courses are impacting large numbers of students. When you affect 5,000 students in an introductory chemistry course, you make a very significant impact. Penn State has discovered that if it redesigns just three courses, it will affect every freshman on campus. Many of these projects are building on what others have done, making additions or improvements based on their particular student populations. As these new techniques are tried, what is learned from the students can be fed back into the design of the course. The faculty can collaboratively and continuously improve both the products and the services that they offer. That, to me, is a big part of what transformation in higher education is all about.

ENDNOTES

1. Schulman, Lee, "Taking Learning Seriously," keynote address from annual American Association of Higher Education meeting, March 1998.

6

WHERE THE RUBBER MEETS THE ROAD: AN ON-CAMPUS PERSPECTIVE OF A CIO

—*Donald Spicer*
UNIVERSITY SYSTEM OF MARYLAND

Continuing our bottom-up review of the impact of e-learning on higher education, it is time for us to walk in the shoes of the campus executive on whose shoulders this entire phenomenon rests: the chief information officer (CIO). As the role of technology on campus has changed from supporting a limited number of administrative units to enabling a campus-wide IT environment, the responsibilities, status and even existence of a university CIO position has grown exponentially. Indeed, 62 percent of chief technology administrators reported to their institution's president in 2001, up from 47.4 percent in 1997.

For e-learning to work—indeed, e-business, e-admissions, e-alumni relations and all other "e–"s as well—the right technology needs to be in place and function smoothly, with high levels of support. Faculty, students, staff, administrators, and others on campus take for granted high-speed Internet connectivity, computers in every lab and lounge, dial-up access for off-campus constituencies, a robust dot-edu Web presence, and more. Given the complexity of the modern CIO's role, they shouldn't.

As we think about the impact of e-learning at institutions of higher education, the view of the CIO working to support technology can be as insightful as that of the faculty member seeking to employ it in the classroom. The priorities of a CIO often reflect the current uses of Internet technologies, and the challenges that keep CIOs up at night suggest what the future might look like.

In this chapter, Donald Spicer outlines for the reader the key "levers" most CIOs manage as e-learning explodes on campus. He makes clear that the backbone of a technology infrastructure consists of more than desktop computers, servers, and software. It includes people, policies, organization, and above all else, expectation setting. We are in what many techno-visionaries and frequent computer users alike consider to be the "dark ages" of IT. Computers crash, Internet access slows, complexities in user interface slow adoption, and the cost of IT is forcing

a digital divide. For e-learning to work, the CIO's opera-
tions must work. Spicer's chapter explains why.

Donald Spicer is in his third career as an academi-
cian. His first career was as a teaching/research faculty
member at a number of institutions, most notably 16
years in the Mathematics Department at Vassar College.
His second career was as a general academic adminis-
trator. His current career is as an academic administra-
tor focusing on issues related to the use of technology in
support of higher education. In this role, he has been Di-
rector of Academic Computing at Dartmouth College,
Assistant Provost for University Computing at the Univer-
sity of Notre Dame, Associate Provost for Information
Technology at Vanderbilt University, and currently Asso-
ciate Vice Chancellor for Information Technology and CIO
at the University System of Maryland. His current posi-
tion is one of developing strategies and implementation
plans for technology-based, mission-critical activities
that transcend individual campuses in the 13-institution
University System. He has a BA (Math and Physics) as
well as a PhD (Math) from the University of Minnesota.
He also has an MA (Math) from Columbia University and
a DiplCS from Corpus Christi College of Cambridge Uni-
versity. He has served on the customer advisory boards
for Apple Computer and IBM, and is currently on the Mi-
crosoft Higher Education Advisory Board. His recent
activities include participation in anytime/anywhere

learning activities related to the Sloan Foundation Asyn-chronous Learning Networks initiative. Additionally, he lectures and consults on issues related to changes in higher education due to the availability of new tools in communications and information management.

I t has been commonly said that the ideal learning environment is a student on one end of a log and Socrates on the other end. That, of course, is not a scalable model. Consequently, in contemporary universities the educational environment involves much more than just the interaction between faculty and students. It involves processes for admitting, advising, and registering; processes for carrying on various commerce activities involving payment of tuition and fees, buying books, and financial aid; activities aimed at developing a sense of community and people-to-people networks; and, finally, career planning and job placement. As a result of the growing complexity of the modern university, IT has evolved into a strategic component of any campus-based program. This is true not only for supporting the administrative units of an institution—enabling anywhere/anytime student services—but the core of the teaching and learning activities on campus as well. Hence the rise of e-learning.

Whether used to supplement traditional classroom instruction or enable distance learning, e-learning reflects the use of IT in direct support of the core mission pursued by higher education institutions. Whereas the previous chapters in this book describe the context for the interaction between changes in higher education and the Internet, this chapter exposes the reader to the day-to-day components of making change possible. At the end of the day, industry trends, market data, capitalization, and course redesign are all useful data points. However, success or failure in effecting change through e-learning, as in most activities, will depend on implementation. As a result, I discuss the factors that make a difference where the rubber meets the road—on campus. My discussion approaches the issues from the perspective of a CIO, one who must consider at the institutional level the technological underpinnings and support necessary for successful implementation and evolution of a technology-based learning environment.

To aid the reader as I step into the world of a CIO, this chapter is organized around three major sections. In the first, I consider the issues of people, organizational structure, financial resources, and policies. In the second, I delve into details and tackle the issues of software, hardware, data, and technology standards. Once the reader is exposed to the key issues a CIO must manage (e.g., financial capabilities, institutional priorities) I close with a specific discussion of University of Maryland University College (UMUC), one of the leading online university programs in the world.

PEOPLE, ORGANIZATIONAL STRUCTURE, FINANCIAL RESOURCES, AND POLICIES

Historically, institutions have had an academic computing organization to support their teaching, learning, and research missions, and an administrative computing organization to support the management of the institution. Often these reported through different lines. Typically, academic computing reported to the provost, and administrative computing to the Vice President for Administration and Finance. This approach reflected a frame of mind that considered these organizations as having parallel and relatively nonoverlapping sets of responsibilities. This may have been true in a centralized, mainframe-oriented world, but in the distributed, network-based technology environments in which most enterprises, including higher education institutions, now find themselves, it is anything but correct organizational or technical design. Data, applications, services, and support are intrinsically intertwined.

In the contemporary institutional organization structure, academic computing and administrative computing, together with telecommunications and media services, have all been combined into a single organization led by a CIO. Although these activities still continue, it is likely that the campus IT organization has been sliced and diced into a cluster of new collaborative entities.

FACULTY SUPPORT

The environment that supports e-learning is important, but in the end, the concepts, organization of knowledge, and mentoring that constitute instruction and create learning opportunities come from the faculty. If teaching and learning are going to evolve into new modes, faculty must lead the way. Yet, given the multiple demands and mixed messages regarding priorities that the majority of faculty face at most traditional institutions, any significant adoption of new approaches by faculty members will require clarification of priorities by the institution and support.

There are many interrelated elements at play here, some of which may be influenced by a CIO and some, such as the relative institutional priority of innovation in teaching and research, must come from other institutional leadership. Those that a CIO can influence include the choice, implementation, integration, and support of tools and services that enable technology-based teaching and learning. These include communication services (e.g., email, messaging, and conferencing systems); easy-to-use online course development and management systems; assurance that infrastructure, policy, and access issues have been addressed; and, finally, integration of all of these systems and services so that the work inherent in managing a class and these services requires a minimum amount of manual labor by individual faculty members.

Even under these circumstances, many faculty members will require substantial support services, some in the nature of usual end-user support—how to effectively use the various tools as well as troubleshooting when things don't work as expected. Others are much more specialized. Teaching electronically is not the same as teaching person-to-person in a classroom setting. There are many pedagogical issues that must be addressed in understanding the new learning medium. Examples include learning how to teach without the visual clues that humans use to understand when effective communication is occurring, how to design class materials so that the learning environment is manageable by the learner without immediate access to the teacher, how to convey complex ideas that have subtle nuances without direct interaction, and so on. A related, but critical issue is that of assessment. At a distance, it is not assured exactly who is responding to questions. Many of these issues are effectively research issues related to teaching at a distance. Some still apply when technology is used to supplement place-based education as well.

When reflecting on all of the factors involved, the current expectation, which is based on the implementation of full online courses, is probably too demanding for many faculty members. The investment necessary to conceive, develop, and offer the equivalent of an entire course online is substantial, and only the most committed faculty members will step up to it in the near future. The implications of this are discussed later in the chapter in the context of technology standards.

The time demands of offering a course online are a substantial and legitimate concern of faculty. With classroom instruction, the faculty commitment to direct interaction with students is typically 150 minutes a week in class and four or five hours a week of office hours. Electronic communication makes the faculty member potentially on-call 24 hours a day, seven days a week. As a learning support model there are many advantages. Students can have questions answered and issues clarified almost immediately, as opposed to waiting for the next class or office hours. However, a faculty member has to learn how to provide that learning benefit without total commitment of personal and professional time and to set appropriate expectations among students. One approach is to move the class dynamic from teacher-centered to a peer-to-peer model, where students help each other learn under the mentorship of the teacher.

TECHNICAL STAFF

The ability of an institution to deal with many of the issues just outlined ultimately will devolve to having the staff who can conceptualize solutions, develop or buy appropriate technologies, integrate various technology services, maintain the overall technology environment, and train and support the user community in the effective use of the available technology services.

In doing this, higher education institutions must increasingly compete with commercial entities that have adopted many of the technologies that have long been in use in higher education. This is a result of the universal adoption of the Internet and Internet standards. As a result, higher education institutions will have to be much more creative in the recruitment and retention of staff with critical skills. Although institutions are used to dealing with the fact that Business professors command higher salaries than English professors, this attitude often hasn't extended to staff. Higher education isn't used to midyear raises, signing bonuses, project milestone bonuses, recruitment rewards, and all of the things available to staff in the technology marketplace. Higher education has sold itself as an interesting work environment with a high quality of life and long-term security. Some of those inducements might still work, but only for certain staff. Higher education institutions have to think much more strategically about technical staff, some of whom want more immediate financial rewards, whereas others might still want stability. Successful institutions will recognize that in this, as in so many things having to do with technology, one size does not fit all.

POLICIES, COPYRIGHT, AND INTELLECTUAL PROPERTY

Today's distributed networked computing environment has many interdependencies that require appropriate policies for effective management. There are also multiple laws regarding privacy of information, management of licenses, and use of copyrighted materials that must be respected. These issues have been amplified as use of the network in support of learning has increased.

Higher education institutions have always pushed the envelope in the use of technology. The fact that many members of a campus community are the youngest, most willing to experiment, and most likely to be technologically adept raises special policy issues. An additional element is that students in many cases use their personal computers, but also use an institutional network in accessing on-campus and off-campus resources. They may feel that what they do with their computers is a personal decision, but in reality it has institutional implications. In this environment, without clearly understood policies, institutions will always be fighting fires without a framework in which to do so. Management policies run counter to the academic culture in this area, but institutions must take a proactive stance that respects the culture of the institution.

One major policy issue that e-learning has brought to the fore is that of ownership of intellectual property. Universities have long recognized that creating knowledge is one of their missions. More precisely, faculty members have been creators of knowledge as a component of their positions within the university. Traditionally, in cases where there were recognized financial implications, such as patents and writing textbooks, there have been institutional policies regarding ownership rights and sharing of revenue. Typically, institutions took no interest in ownership of textbook rights, but negotiated case-by-case agreements relating to potential revenues from patentable intellectual properties.

Online learning has introduced significant new issues into the matter of relative ownership and has raised questions regarding the exact implications of the status of faculty members as employees and as teacher-scholars. When teaching was a classroom activity, institutions provided the students and classrooms, and managed the business issues related to all components of the instructional system. Faculty members were happy to fit into this system and do what they did best—organize and communicate information and mentor students. In the e-learning world all of these conditions are subject to change. Commercial, for-profit vehicles are available to faculty as outlets for conveying knowledge. On the other side, institutions can disaggregate the components of offering a course, separating course design from course offering. In sum, the cottage industry of an individual faculty member developing and offering a custom course for each class of 30 or so students need not be the only model, or even the predominant model, in the future.

The flip side of the intellectual property issue is that of copyright. Few, if any, courses are fully self-sufficient, depending only on the instructor's own materials. In a classroom-focused, paper-based model there have been long-standing traditions based on books and governed by copyright to manage rights to use materials. This was challenged by technology 40 years ago with the rise of copy machines. The doctrine of fair use has been continually tested by case law, ranging from issues related to individual students copying materials, to copies on reserve in libraries, to the creation of "course packs" of materials from different publishers bundled together by the instructor and made available at campus copy centers. Online learning again stands to provide new challenges to appropriate use of others' intellectual property. The Digital Millennium Copyright Act of 1998 attempts to define appropriate use in the digital era, but clear definition in operational terms remains a work in progress, and case law challenges are just beginning to occur. Assuming individual faculty members and course designers wish to do the right thing and universities wish to advise them appropriately, much still needs to be clarified to be able to accomplish these objectives.

FINANCING CAMPUS TECHNOLOGY

IT has challenged many traditional modes of doing business in higher education institutions. Financing IT has perhaps been more of a challenge than anything else mentioned in the chapter to this point. Technology is expensive, it changes rapidly, investments lose value quickly, and staffs require salaries that are out of line with staffing in other areas. This does not mesh well with budget processes that expect stability and are often created up to two years before expenditures are made. It is a challenge for the CIO to plan and manage in such an environment and a challenge for institutions to accommodate an activity so far out of the norm.

Corporations have faced the same challenge, but they can justify the cost of technology in terms of improved productivity or they can improve customer services and pass the costs on to the customer. Higher education often lacks such vehicles. Productivity in an educational context is difficult to measure, if valued at all. Passing costs on to customers may be impossible in public higher education and may make a private higher education institution less price competitive. It might also increase the cost of financial aid in either setting.

There are several hot-topic financial issues with which most institutions are struggling. A few of these include competition for staff; assuring access for all students, faculty, and staff; and cost of administrative systems that have a life of 15 to 20 years, are hugely expensive, and in many cases now seem to be in need of replacement.

The overarching financial issue is that of *life-cycle budgeting and replacement.* Lurching from replacement crisis to replacement crisis and responding to needs with end-of-year "budget dust" might have sufficed when IT was just another campus service and not strategic. Now that institutions are increasingly dependent on IT for the day-to-day operation of the campus and for success in all mission activities, lack of funding for necessary upgrades and replacements will ultimately be reflected in failure or slow-down in front-line institutional activities. Unfortunately, although the need to change is increasingly being recognized, few institutions have stepped up to budgeting in this manner. In part, this is the result of the inability to recover saved costs from traditional activities and redirect them to the support of new activities. It is also partially due to the fact that IT budgets are widely distributed across campus budgets and decision making is similarly distributed.

TECHNOLOGY INFRASTRUCTURE

NETWORK

The network (i.e., the Internet) is the common theme across the chapters of this book, because it is the major medium on which e-learning is based. It is thus the roadbed of a campus technology infrastructure. Almost every residential campus has networked its residence halls. Indeed, the core campus network has increasingly become a strategic institutional investment. Most institutions have stepped up to installing a pervasive and robust network. However, given the rapid growth in demand for network services, both by members of the campus community and by the applications they use, it is proving to be difficult to have the campus network keep pace—especially with normal academic budgeting approaches. Even the capital components are under stress. The first institutions that invested in pervasive campus networking are now finding that the cable plant, a 15-year investment, is coming to the end of its life. It is likely that fiber to the desktop, which has only been needed in the most extreme research environments, will at some point in the next 15 years be the expectation of each wired user work environment.

It has become a rule of thumb that campus network technologies need to be replaced on a cycle of no more than four years, and research universities must plan for major upgrades on a three-year basis. It is unlikely that this situation will improve over the next decade, and in fact it is likely to grow more complicated. The major push during the past 15 years has been to wire the campus. The next push likely will be to add pervasive wireless capability to data networking. Although there will always be a need for the capability of a wired environment, the trend is toward multiple-access devices and mobility. Pervasive connectivity used to mean at every workplace. In the near future, it will mean everywhere. This will be an enhancement for the traditional campus network, not a replacement. Wireless standards are relatively new and evolving rapidly, so this will create substantial capital, maintenance, and support challenges for campus CIOs.

Related to networks at the center of enabling the e-learning programs of tomorrow is a trend that has been much discussed but only now is coming to fruition: convergence of voice, video, and data. Convergence has been long awaited and it has organizational, infrastructure, and service implications. Often, telecommunications has been perceived to be a business service of a campus, whereas media services and data networking have been used as academic support services. Telecommunications is frequently seen as a profit center, whereas data networking and media service have been cost centers, perhaps with some charge-back mechanism. Also, traditionally telecommunication services have been provided over their own dedicated cable plant, as have data networking and video services, if video was delivered over a network. In the emerging model, these services will all coexist over a common cable plant. This convergence might reduce costs, though as with all transitions, multiple approaches will coexist for a period of years. Also, there are substantial sunk costs in the historic telecommunications infrastructure that cannot be easily recovered.

Navigating the technical and organizational changes attendant to convergence will be a challenge for campus CIOs. At campuses without CIOs the issues may proceed without direction and coordination.

Beyond the campus, institutions have provided dial-up service for nonresidential students as well as faculty and staff who work at home. This is a historic anomaly, resulting from the fact that the Internet started as an academic service; one had to be affiliated with an academic institution to gain Internet access in the 1980s and early 1990s. In the absence of commercial alternatives, higher education institutions developed access strategies for both on-campus and off-campus communities, which has proven to be unsupportable in a climate where everyone wants access all of the time. Increasingly, institutions are telling their communities that they need to turn to the marketplace for Internet access. That students, faculty, and staff have had a "no-charge" (at least to them) environment means that this message isn't always well received. The move to higher bandwidth to the home, which no one expects the campus to provide, will resolve this issue in time.

One implication of outsourcing remote Internet access is that a much more sophisticated approach to authorization to licensed services needs to be developed. This issue is discussed later in the chapter in the section dealing with middleware. Direct authenticated campus dial-in has the benefit of assigning a campus Internet Protocol (IP) address to the remote user. A simple filtering of access using this IP address can suffice to assure limited access to licensed materials. With users increasingly depending on Internet service providers for Internet access from home, when such a user tries to access campus-licensed materials, he or she would be rejected as coming from an off-campus address. Thus, license management will require a more sophisticated authorization mechanism than IP address filtering.

Ironically, the various networking trends described in this section are putting campuses in a surprising situation. The institutions that have long been fully networked may now find that they have the poorest cable plant and are struggling to maintain capabilities demanded by a university community. On the other hand, the institutions that have struggled to fully network their campuses may now have the "latest and greatest." Similarly, institutions that have kept their telecommunications switch current may find they cannot justify the risks inherent in converged technologies for several years, but an institution that has to now replace its outdated switch during this transition period may find that it is effective in the long run to invest now in voice-over IP, the fully converged model.

DATA MANAGEMENT

In addition to physical networks, the other commonly accepted component of infrastructure is that of institutional data and the enterprise applications used to manage that data. The new applications that manage the enterprise information and access to that information are generally termed enterprise resource planning (ERP) applications. These complex systems can be distributed across multiple servers. Although this approach is much more flexible and convenient, it has significant implications in terms of security, implementation approaches, and support.

Traditionally, major software applications were implemented and run on central hardware, but access tended to be via direct connection, limited as a result to a relatively small number of administrators and data entry personnel. With the coming of the network, the design stayed the same, but computers replaced terminals. With truly pervasive campus networking and Web browsers widely understood and universally available, the newest generation of applications is built around a self-service model that empowers each member of the campus community to access his or her own personal information. This, in turn, has implications in terms of uses of data and support. Additionally, by interfacing this data with a wide range of services, such as communication (e.g., email and asynchronous conferencing), library (electronic information resources), and learning (online course management environments), this enterprise data can manage authentication and authorization capabilities to such services. Such an integrated approach reduces the overhead in services to both the providers and consumers. More will be said of this later in this chapter.

ASSURING ACCESS

No self-service infrastructure or e-learning program has much impact if students, faculty, and staff cannot access it. Thus, assured access, particularly for students, has become an institutional, and even a national, mantra. It is one face of the so-called digital divide. Resolution can take many forms. In some cases, it might mean establishing adequate publicly accessible workstations. This model is not normally sustainable as institutions move toward greater reliance on technology in the curriculum, pervasive use of electronic communication tools, and self-service enterprise applications. An alternative is to develop mechanisms to encourage personal ownership of computers and other network-capable devices. Although the cost of these devices keeps dropping, it is difficult to meet the needs of those who cannot afford a computer or necessary network access. Some institutions are requiring computer ownership, which forces the institution to formalize a strategy for meeting the needs of all students and allows the purchase of a computer to qualify under financial aid guidelines.

From the CIO's perspective, there are many implications of this issue. Maintaining the currency and availability of institutional public access areas is a substantial financial investment. Ideally, hardware should be upgraded on a three- to four-year cycle. Additionally, there is increasing need to keep some facilities open on a 24-hour-a-day basis. As private ownership of PCs becomes pervasive, the need for institutional public areas might decrease, but it will not disappear. There will always be a need for higher capability equipment or specialized software that might be beyond the abilities of individuals to acquire. Also, many students will own desktop computers, which will be kept in their residence. Those students will depend on institutional resources when away from their residence.

Complicating this issue is the multiplicity of devices that constantly appear on campus. Access to learning or institutional resources no longer requires a traditional computer. The current variations range from portable computers to personal digital assistants to Internet-aware telephone devices. In the near term there will be e-book readers, some of which also will have wireless Web browsing capabilities. Other mobile devices will certainly be developed. Designing services that can be displayed on all of these devices will become an important issue. Support demands will similarly increase. If worrying about cross-platform support for Wintel, Mac, and UNIX has been a headache, the emerging platform environment will make that appear prosaic.

TECHNOLOGY STANDARDS

In e-learning, there are many components that need to work together. It is unlikely that the best of breed can be purchased from a single vendor that can make them all work together in an integrated manner. Technical staff may be able to use documented application program interfaces (APIs) to integrate these components, but without accepted interface standards, this will be time-consuming, expensive labor that will have to be replicated whenever one of the components is upgraded or replaced.

In addition, course content may be compiled in a format specific to a vendor's learning management system (LMS), which is likely to be proprietary. Without appropriate standards, if the institution or faculty member chooses to move the content to another vendor's LMS, it might find that the content is captured by the initial encapsulation. Accepted standards for packaging content can resolve this matter.

In addition to packaging, discovery of content is another driver of standards. Traditionally, the unit of instruction has been the course. A faculty member is expected to develop and deliver a defined number of courses to students. Sometimes this is done in a team-teaching mode and sometimes, especially in large multisection courses, there may be a standard curriculum template developed by a department. Much of the thought regarding how to parse the learning environment has been carried over to e-learning. This has caused a significant barrier to the creation of online courses: Faculty members have to step up to the requirements inherent in developing everything themselves. If there were standards for finding and integrating more finely defined components created by others, then faculty members could concentrate on the overall conception of the online course, creating those components for which they had the expertise and capability to do so, and using components created by others to fill out the rest of the offering. Of course, there are intellectual property rights and commerce issues at stake here as well. The analogs in a traditional medium might be that of the course pack or reserve shelf in the library where sections or chapters of material from many independent sources are made available. In the online world, this may be extended to simulations, animations, video segments, and so forth.

Many of the standards for the online learning environment described here are being developed by the Instructional Management System (IMS) Project, originally part of the EDUCOM (now Educause) National Learning Infrastructure Initiative (NLII). The IMS Project has become a totally self-sufficient nonprofit entity. It has a substantial number of educational, corporate, and content provider members. More details can be found at *www.imsproject.org*.

TYING THINGS TOGETHER—PORTALS
AND MIDDLEWARE

A distributed networked environment has many components. There are emerging technologies that will help make
these components more usable as a whole. Increasingly,
end-user access to technologies and services is handled
using a World Wide Web browser. The institutional access
point to enterprise information or services has been the
home page. A home page can have links to other pages and
services, but the concept has many inherent limitations.
Home pages are typically passive (i.e., one has to actively
seek out and "go to" that page), and are designed to provide
a view of the institution that tries to meet the needs of all
possible viewers. What is needed is a vehicle that can be
personalized by each viewer, showing just the information
and services the individual viewer wishes to see on a regular basis. Additionally, that information should be available
in an active manner, as appropriate. For example, when it
is updated, the new information should be immediately
published to all subscribing viewers' browser interfaces.
This active, personalizable interface is called a *portal*. Although the portal concept is still undergoing full definition,
and tools for developing portals are either proprietary or
limited to only a specific vendor's information or services,
it is increasingly accepted that the more useful portal

concept will supplement and, perhaps in the long run, supplant home pages.

Equally important as the portal's look and feel is the class of technologies that identify users, authorize their access to services, and provide security in an online environment. This class of technologies is called *middleware*. The emerging distributed networked environment requires thinking about an information and services architecture rather than just thinking in terms of everything being provided by a monolithic shared computer. Middleware can be considered the electronic glue that keeps track of people and network resources in a distributed environment and manages the ability of people to find and use the resources to which they are entitled. This also entails providing security as necessary. Security itself has many components, from securing the infrastructure to protecting data, as well as assuring those who use electronic resources that their transmissions are not observed or tampered with, they are conversing with whom they think they are, and the recipient is assured that the sender is who they say they are.

ELECTRONIC INFORMATION RESOURCES

Much as the physical library is the heart of the campus in traditional educational environments, the electronic library can be the foundation on which e-learning is built. The chance that the physical library will disappear completely is highly unlikely. The accumulated holdings of the Library of Congress, for example, would take half a century to digitize according to most estimates. To date, electronic resources have been best available in disciplines that use the most current publications as core materials (i.e., journals in medicine, mathematics, science, and engineering). The more that conversion is required, the less likely that electronic materials will be available is a rule of thumb for the foreseeable future. Additionally, the cost for fully digitizing a collection of 19th-century science is staggering, even if academically necessary. The more reasonable assumption is that because new materials are generally created electronically, they can be stored and delivered electronically. However, who can retrieve information created in 1983 with an outdated software application such as the spreadsheet product VisiCalc and stored on a 5.25-inch floppy disk? Thus there are some fundamental issues related to archiving that need to be addressed before society can depend on a fully digital library as the only information repository.

INSTITUTIONS THAT GO BEYOND THE ENVELOPE

To this point, my observations in this chapter have generally applied to the "typical" institution that is trying to use current IT effectively in support of its e-learning activities. Within the University System of Maryland (USM), where I serve as System CIO, there is one institution in particular that is pushing the envelope in using IT to support of new models of teaching and learning: the University of Maryland University College (UMUC; *www.umuc.edu*). Although it serves many adult learners in Maryland via distributed centers around the state, and many adult learners at military bases around the world, its high-growth strategic direction is to expand its offering of online instruction. Currently, with 60,000 online course registrations in the spring term of 2001, UMUC may be one of the largest online institutions in the world. The interesting question for this discussion is what the implications are of being online at that scale.

In addition to the fact that most students never come to the UMUC "campus," most faculty members rarely come there either. "Campus" is in quotes because the main campus consists of two buildings in College Park, Maryland, one of which also is a 100-room inn and conference center. Questions immediately arise regarding quality assurance in instruction, uniformity in course offerings, and so on. Because those are academic questions and this chapter is focusing on the technology and support issues related to the impact of the network on education, these topics are left for discussion elsewhere.

The model at UMUC calls for full-time faculty to work with course designers at the UMUC headquarters to develop the online courses in a template form. Many of the faculty who deliver the instruction are professionals in a related discipline and often are adjunct faculty members. They typically are nonresident to Maryland, but many have a long-term association with UMUC in faculty roles. Before they teach their first course for UMUC they must go through a six-week training course themselves. Part of the instruction is directed toward learning the tools necessary to teach online, but the great majority of it is aimed at pedagogy in an online mode: How does one communicate effectively online? How does one know that ideas are getting across effectively without the puzzled looks that an instructor depends on in the classroom? How does one structure peer-to-peer discussions rather than just instructor-to-class presentations? How does one deal with cultural differences when the class participants are from multiple countries? How does one maintain momentum in a class when the discussion of a topic may spread over a period of several days due to the asynchronous character of multi-time-zone e-learning? These are challenging issues with which UMUC has significant experience.

Support for faculty who are at a distance themselves poses a unique problem for the institution. Some of it can be addressed with easy-to-use tools, much from training; in the end, support comes from having effective help-desk and support services. That faculty members are worldwide means that these services have to be fully available 24 hours a day. Recognizing the necessity of this and the difficulty of supporting this approach with fully internal staff and other resources, UMUC has outsourced part of its helpdesk services. A business that is organized for worldwide support covers incoming questions after the normal working day in Maryland.

Many institutions can control most of the necessary network infrastructure on campus. When most students are off campus, coming in via various local Internet service providers, the quality of a connection to the Internet, and thus to the course, becomes a much more difficult issue. One needs to plan strategies that assume the worst, which means either designing necessary access requirements to the lowest level acceptable or designing so that the service level can be set to the available bandwidth and quality of service. The former is limiting in design and disadvantages the student with good service, whereas the latter may require multiple design, implementation, and maintenance approaches.

If one intends to have students participating in courses on a global scale, then the course Web server and services need to meet the conflicting requirements of appearing "local" to the student, no matter where the student accesses the materials, and being the same for all students. UMUC accomplishes this by having servers in the U.S., Europe, and Asia and using infrastructure software that synchronizes data across remote servers.

As implied earlier, the global orientation essentially forces course discussions to be asynchronous because scheduling synchronous discussions may be impossible. Another USM institution, University of Maryland Biotechnical Institute (UMBI), offers instruction in Scandinavia on a synchronous basis through the Collaborative Virtual University Education Program, VIRTUE (*www.umbi.umd.edu/virtue/*). Given that there are only two time zones involved, although admittedly five hours apart, this can be handled by careful scheduling. This approach wouldn't be convenient if the time spread were any greater.

To support the investments that are needed to be successful, UMUC has to run as much like a global business as a traditional higher education institution. There are some immediate implications of this—growing tuition revenues and creating access to financial markets. In the former instance, UMUC cannot hope to raise prices adequately to fund the infrastructure that will support its future. Thus, like a business, it views infrastructure investments (IT rather than buildings) as being recouped by rapid growth in enrollments. To date the UMUC leadership has successfully walked the narrow line between growing fast enough to pay back investments and not growing so fast that it can't provide a quality educational experience. During the years 1999 through 2001, their online enrollments have tended to grow in the 150 percent to 200 percent range semester by semester.

As one can imagine, it is difficult to support this model from state appropriations, endowment, and tuition alone. In fact, UMUC receives a relatively small state appropriation, largely directed toward its services to Maryland residents. Similarly, it has a negligible endowment. As a result, UMUC must bring a disciplined perspective to analyzing the cost and return in the online business. UMUC found early on that to offer a quality educational experience, they could not let online class sizes to get too large. Thus scaling up tends to involve opening new sections of a course, not making the existing one larger. The cost and return of adding sections folded in with the cost of developing the course in the first place requires careful analysis—much more careful than in the usual higher education environment, which places less concern on financial return on investment.

MODELS FOR ADDRESSING ISSUES

The traditional model for higher education institutions is to focus on the variable costs of an activity and not on existing fixed costs. This leads to a mindset expressed as "We have the staff already, but not the budgets to hire consultants, so let's do it ourselves." This could be a matter of economics, a matter of hubris, or a sense that the marketplace offers options that are too conservative for their perceived needs. Technology has become so complex and expectations have grown beyond the ability to meet them in traditional ways, forcing a rethinking on many campuses of how to balance resources and needs. To seriously be in the e-learning business, institutions will have to evaluate core competencies and strategic activities in ways that they might never have had to do before. Most likely, an institution will want to maintain control of truly strategic activities and not turn them over to an outside contracted entity. However, if the activity is not strategic and might be better done by an organization to which this activity is core business, it is likely to be profitable to negotiate a service level agreement provided externally.

As mentioned earlier, UMUC did this with after-hours help-desk services. Institutions might wish to evaluate technical services, which could be provided by a commercial entity without the institution itself having to compete in the job market for technical staff. An example might be managing servers. If an institution is in the e-learning business, who cares where the servers are located and who hires systems staff to manage them, as long as they are well-situated on the Internet, with good network peering capabilities, and the staff is competent and available on a 24/7 basis? There is no competitive advantage in doing this internally.

An example of outsourcing in a different mode, also from among the University System of Maryland institutions, may be instructive. The University of Baltimore (*www.ubalt.edu*) decided to offer an online MBA program to complement its traditional MBA program offered to regional students. The institution and its faculty decided in 1999 that there was a market opportunity for an appropriate degree program, which they wished to capture. However, to do so, they needed to move with some dispatch. Yet, although they had commitment from sufficient faculty members to proceed, the institution did not have the technical, course design, or support capabilities to properly develop and offer such a program. Rather than trying to develop the capabilities internally or limping along, the University of Baltimore contracted with an online service provider to work with the faculty and the institution to get the program underway. They were able to offer the first courses within nine months and were able to develop the entire degree program in a dove-tailed manner, which allowed the first students to graduate in two years. The vendor not only worked on the campus, but also hosted the courses on their servers in an Application Service Provider (ASP) model. Faculty members simply had to develop the text-based materials, and ship them off to the vendor. The materials were converted into the online format supported by the vendor and installed on servers. The University of Baltimore feels that they were able to proceed more rapidly and had more satisfied faculty and students than a traditional internal model would have allowed. The contract is expected to break even within two years. This may be considered an example of fully outsourcing those components of e-learning that do not fit the skill set of an institution with an expertise of presentation in classrooms. Of course, although the faculty didn't have to worry about putting materials online, they did have to learn how to teach in an online course environment. The vendor assisted with that training as well.

SUMMARY

In this chapter, I have outlined a wide-ranging list of issues that any institution wishing to take effective advantage of the opportunities offered by the Internet in improving teaching and learning as well as the operation of the institution must address. There are some models for addressing these issues by IT leadership teams, but the current most effective approach is to bring all of the components under the purview of a single IT leader, the CIO. Most institutions are heavily investing in IT with the hope of improving current processes or extending the programs of the institution to new learners in new ways. Although the idea of getting into the distance-education business is widely held, there are many necessary components for success. An institution should fully understand the implications before moving too aggressively into an entirely new line of business.

7

QUESTIONING MEDIA

—Neil Postman
NEW YORK UNIVERSITY

As we near its conclusion, this book has spent the lion's share of its effort exploring the degree to which the impact of the Internet on higher education is transformative or evolutionary. A key assumption of the question is that some form of impact is being made, regardless of its magnitude. Missing from the question is a consideration of whether any amount of influence is desirable at all. Although one might consider it axiomatic that any use of Internet technologies heralds with it some degree of change in the teaching and learning process, it is far from clear that we should welcome the change, arguing over degree only, without questioning the fundamental meaning of change.

In this chapter, we reserve time to question. To be more precise, we examine six questions, posed with the skeptical pen of professor and author Neil Postman. By stepping back from the top-down and bottom-up consideration of e-learning in higher education, Postman challenges us to consider the virtues of technology and media in our society more broadly, albeit with special consideration to e-learning, as it is the subject of this book. Through the questions he poses, Postman applies a different lens to the growth of e-learning. For example, rather than simply accepting the simplicity of using traditional metaphors to explain e-learning activities—for example, describing a chat tool as a "virtual classroom"—Postman forces the reader to consider the true qualitative differences between typing messages into text boxes and engaging in a classroom dialogue with a professor and peers. Whether the reader agrees with his subjective belief that the answer is "no" is not the point of the chapter. That the reader recognizes the importance of questioning the fundamental role that technology continues to play in our lives certainly is the point.

Neil Postman received his Doctoral Degree from Columbia University and has taught at New York University (NYU) for 38 years. He is the Paulette Goddard Professor of Media Ecology and Chair of the Department of Culture *and Communications at NYU. He is the author of 20 books including* Language in America, Teaching as a Subversive Activity *(with Charles Weingartner),* The Disappearance of Childhood, Conscientious Objections, *and* Amusing Our-selves to Death. *His articles, of which more than 200 have been published, have appeared in the* New York Times Magazine, The Atlantic, Harper's, Time Magazine, The Sat-urday Review, The Harvard Education Review, The Wash-ington Post, *and* Le Monde. *He is on the editorial board of* The Nation *magazine. He has lectured all over the world, and in 1985, gave the keynote address at the Frankfurt Book Fair. In 1986, Postman was given the George Orwell Award for Clarity in Language by the National Council of Teachers of English. For 10 years, he was editor of* Et Cetera, *the journal of General Semantics. He is the holder of the Christian Lindback Award for excellence in teach-ing. In 1988, he was given the Distinguished Professor Award by NYU. His more recent books (for Knopf and Viking, respectively) are* Technopoly *and* How to Watch Television News *(with Steve Powers). In the spring of 1991, he was the Lawrence Lombard Visiting Professor of The Press and Public Policy at the John F. Kennedy School of Government at Harvard University. In 1995, Knopf pub-lished his book,* The End of Education, *which in its Italian edition won the equivalent of our National Book Award. In 1999, Knopf published his* Building a Bridge to the 18th Century.

This chapter addresses six key questions about technology and media, answers to which might provide some insights into the ways e-learning may intrude itself into our institutions of education. As a disclaimer, although the answers to these questions are important, they will vary according to who is answering. If, for example, you are in the business of selling technology to educators, your answers might be different from those of a teacher or parent. The journey is in the asking.

Before addressing the six questions, I wish to make two central points, one clarifying what I will be arguing, and the other, why I am arguing it. First, in this chapter I make a distinction between a technology and a medium. As I see it, a technology is to a medium as the brain is to a mind. Like the mind, a medium is a use to which a physical apparatus is put. A technology becomes a medium as it is given a place in a particular social setting, as it insinuates itself into economic and political contexts. A technology, in other words, is merely a machine, a piece of hard-wiring. As has been written by many scholars, a medium is a social creation.

It is useful to make this distinction, because with it we can more easily understand how a technology such as e-learning is used by any particular culture, and how it is used is not necessarily the only way it could be used. For example, if Americans try to answer the question, "what is television?" we have to understand that we're not talking about television as a technology, but television as a medium. There are many places in the world where television, although the same technology as it is in America, is an entirely different medium from the one Americans know. I refer to places where the majority of people do not have television sets, or where only one station is available, or where television doesn't operate around the clock, or where most programs have as their purpose the direct furtherance of government policy, or where commercials are unknown. In such places, television will not have the same meaning or power as it does in America, which is to say, it is possible for a technology to be used so that its social, economic, and political consequences are quite different from one culture to another.

Of course, like the brain itself, every technology has an inherent bias, both unique technical limitations and possibilities. That is to say, every technology has embedded in its physical form a predisposition to being used in certain ways and not others, and only those who know nothing of the history of technology believe that a technology is entirely neutral or adaptable. Indeed, here's an old joke that mocks such a naive belief: Thomas Edison, the joke goes, would have revealed his discovery of the electric light a lot sooner than he did, except for the fact that every time he turned it on he held it to his mouth and said, "Hello?" You can't use an electric light to speak to your mother in

Boston, and you can't use a telephone to illuminate a page in a book. In other words, each technology has an agenda of its own, and gives us "instructions," so to speak, on how to fulfill its own technical destiny. We must understand this truism, and we especially must not underestimate it, but we need not be tyrannized by it. We do not always have to go in exactly the direction that a technology leads us toward. We have obligations to ourselves that may supercede our obligations to any technology.

Now, having said all this, I will, for the most part, be using the terms *technology* and *media* nearly interchangeably, because as Americans, we are all familiar with the uses we make of our various technologies. Nonetheless, I hope you, the reader, will keep the distinction between these two words in mind, because there are circumstances in which it is thoughtless and even misleading to use them as synonyms.

Now, to my second preparatory point of the chapter, which concerns my own attitude toward technology. I must admit that I do not have much use for email, finding it mostly a distraction. I do not have voice-mail or a cellular phone. I do not use a word processor. I write my books with a pen and yellow pad. And I do not regard Bill Gates as a genius, although I have good reason for each of these deficiencies of mine about which I have written elsewhere. Nonetheless, because of them, I have a reputation as being antitechnology, though I regard it as stupid to be antitechnology. That would be something like being antifood. We need technology to live, as we need food to live, but, of course, if we eat too much food, or eat food that has no nutritional value, or eat food that is infected with disease, we turn a means of survival into its opposite, and the same might be said of the ways in which we use technology. It can be used as life-enhancing, and it can be used as life-diminishing. In any case, it makes no sense to be categorically antitechnology, but it is certainly reasonable to be deeply suspicious of technology, for it's pretty clear that technologies and the media they become can have most serious effects on our ways of living, our values, our social institutions, and our psychic habits. Only a fool would blithely welcome any technology without having given serious thought not only to what the technology will do, but also to what it will undo.

Enough of prologue. Let us now turn to my questions.

WHAT PROBLEM GETS SOLVED BY THIS NEW TECHNOLOGY?

This first question needs to be addressed whenever anyone tells us about a new technology (e.g., interactive television, virtual reality, the Internet, or whatever). The question is: What is the problem to which this technology is a solution? This question needs to be asked, because there are technologies that are not solutions to any problem that a normal person would regard as significant. Although former Vice President Al Gore is certainly a normal person, I am skeptical of the reasons he gave for the nation to spend billions of dollars to develop and create an information superhighway. He has said that the highway will provide each of us with access to 500 or perhaps even 1,000 television stations. I am therefore obliged to ask if this is a problem most of us yearn to have solved. Indeed, need to have solved. Do we believe that having access to 40 or 50 stations, as most of us do, is inadequate, and that we cannot achieve a fulfilled life unless we have 1,000 stations to choose from? What exactly is the problem to be solved here? Whatever it is, we're entitled to ask about it and even to be skeptical about it.

A good example of such skepticism helpfully applied concerned a question raised some years ago, as to whether or not the United States Government should subsidize the manufacture of a supersonic jet. Both the British and French already had built SSTs, and a serious debate ensued in the halls of Congress and elsewhere about whether or not we should have one of our own. And so the question was asked, "What is the problem to which the supersonic jet is the solution?" The answer, it turned out, was that it takes six hours to go from New York to London in a 747; with a supersonic jet, it could be done in three hours. Most Americans, I am happy to say, did not think that that was a sufficiently serious problem to warrant such a heavy investment. Besides, some Americans asked, "What would we do with the three hours we saved?" Their answer was: "We'd probably watch television." The suggestion was thus made that we put TV sets on the 747 and thereby save billions of dollars.

WHOSE PROBLEM IS IT?

After answering the question, "What is the problem to which a particular technology is the solution?," one can ask, "Whose problem is it?" In the case of the SST, the problem of getting to London faster than 747s could was largely a problem for movie stars, rock musicians, and corporate executives. This was hardly a problem that most Americans would regard as worth solving if it would cost them a lot of money. But this question—"Whose problem is it?"—needs to be applied to any technology. Most technologies do solve some problem, but the problem might not be everybody's problem, or even most people's problem. We need to be very careful in determining who will benefit from a technology and who will pay for it. They are not always the same people, particularly in the field of education, where the interests of donors, boards, instructors, and students can vary quite dramatically.

WHAT NEW PROBLEMS ARE CREATED
AFTER SOLVING AN OLD PROBLEM?

Let us say that we have found a technological solution to a problem that most people have. We then come to the third question: "Suppose we solve this problem, and solve it decisively. What new problems will be created *because* we have solved an old problem?" The automobile solves some very important problems for most people, but in doing so has poisoned our air, choked our cities with traffic, and contributed toward the destruction of some of the beauty of our natural landscape. Antibiotics have certainly solved some significant problems for almost all people, but in doing so have resulted in the weakening of our immune systems. In America, television has solved several important problems, but in solving them, it has changed the nature of political discourse, led to a serious decline in literacy, and even made the traditional process of socializing children difficult, if not impossible.

It is doubtful that we can think of any single important technology that did not generate new problems as a result of solving an old problem. Of course, it is sometimes very difficult to know what new problems will arise as a result of a technological solution. Benedictine monks invented the mechanical clock in the 13th century to be more precise in performing their canonical prayers, which they needed to do seven times a day. Had they known that the mechanical clock would eventually be used by merchants as a means of establishing a standardized work day and then a standardized product (i.e., that the clock would be used as an instrument for making money instead of serving God), the monks might have decided that their sundials and water clocks were quite sufficient. Had Gutenberg foreseen that his printing press with movable type would lead to the breakup of the Holy Roman Empire, he surely would have saved his old wine press to make wine and not books.

In the 13th century, perhaps it didn't matter so much if people lacked technological vision. Maybe not even in the 15th century. However, in a technological society like ours, we can no longer afford to move into the future with our eyes tightly closed. We need to speculate in an open-eyed way about negative possibilities. But, as I have said, it is no easy matter to know what sorts of problems a new technology will generate. To produce responsible answers requires knowledge of the history of technology and of technology's social effects and the principles governing technological change; in other words, the kind of knowledge most people do not have, and that our culture, including our corporate culture, has little interest in pursuing.

WHO AND WHAT MIGHT BE HARMED BY A TECHNOLOGICAL SOLUTION?

It is not sufficient to reflect in a general way on the possible costs of technology. To give some focus to our inquiries, we need to ask a fourth question: "Which people and what institutions might be most seriously harmed by a technological solution?" This was the question that gave rise to the Luddite movement in England during the years 1811 to 1818. The people we call Luddites were skilled manual workers in the garment industry at the time when mechanization was taking command and the factory system was being put into place. They knew perfectly well what advantages mechanization would bring to most people, but they also saw, with equal clarity, how it would bring ruin to their own ways of life, especially to their children, who were being employed as virtual slave laborers in factories and mines. They resisted technological change by the simplistic and useless expedient of smashing to bits industrial machinery, which they continued to do until they were imprisoned or killed by the British Army.

No one knows exactly where the word *Luddite* came from, but the word has come to mean a person who resists technological change in any way, and it is usually used as an insult. Why this is so is a bit puzzling to me, because only a fool doesn't know that new technologies always produce winners and losers, and there is nothing irrational about loser resistance.

Bill Gates, who is by most accounts a winner, knows about winning and losing and because he is no fool, his propaganda continuously implies that computer technology can bring harm to no one. That is the way of winners; they want losers to be grateful and enthusiastic and especially to be unaware that they are losers. Given the focus of this book, let us take schoolteachers as an example of losers who are deluded into thinking they are winners. It is clear to me that we need more teachers, and that we ought to pay more to those we have. However, school authorities are resistant to hiring more teachers and to paying them more and they complain continuously about a shortage of funds. The fact is that school authorities are now preparing to spend, in the aggregate, billions of dollars to wire schools to accommodate computer technology for reasons that are by no means clear. To my knowledge, there does not exist any compelling evidence that PCs or any other manifestation of computer technology can do for children what good, well-paid, unburdened teachers can do. Nor is there any evidence whatsoever that children in wired classrooms do any better than children who aren't. So where is the outcry from teachers? They are losers in this deal, and serious losers.

For example, *The Washington Post* reported not too long ago that the state of Maryland planned to provide Internet access to every single one of its 1,262 public schools, at a cost of $53 million. Maryland's governor, Paris Glendening, said in the announcement that this would give all students access to the wide body of information available. Although reviews by national analysts on the use of computers in schools has been mixed, each school was to have at least two terminals linked to the Internet by the first year, and at least three to five terminals linked within five years.

Governor Glendening called this a "bold and big initiative," and expected tens of millions of additional dollars to be donated by private enterprise, so that the total expenditure will be close to $100 million. Here is his justification: "Accessing information is the first, vital step in understanding and ultimately improving the world we live in."

Let us put aside the fact that, at best, this is a problematic claim, and at worst, errant nonsense. I would remind you of Henry David Thoreau's observation that "all our inventions are but improved means of unimproved ends."[2] Let us also put aside the fact that even if the governor's claim is true, American students already have an oversupply of sources of information and do not a require $1 million investment to be well-informed citizens. Putting all that aside, can we agree that the following alternative statement would be happier news and more rational for both teachers and students?

> The state of Maryland seems to think so, since it committed to spending $100 million toward increasing its number of students, paying the teachers it has higher salaries, and reducing the teaching loads. Governor Glendening said the motive was to give the students a more creative, attentive, and wholesome educational environment.

I should think most teachers would support such an investment, but we hear very little from them on this score. In fact, many teachers are thrilled by the thought of school authorities spending millions on computer terminals.

ARE CHANGES GAINED AND LOST WITH NEW TECHNOLOGIES?

Here is a fifth question: "What changes in language are being enforced by new technologies, and what is being gained and lost by such changes?" I feel sure that most will agree with that no matter what new media come into our lives, language will remain our most indispensable medium, and it's always a serious matter when new meanings arise or old ones are lost. Think, for example, of how the words *community* and *conversation* are now employed by those who use the Internet, especially for e-learning. Or think of how television has changed the meaning of the phrase, *political debate,* the word *public,* and the term *participatory democracy.* Not so long ago, Lawrence Grossman wrote a book called *The Electronic Republic,* in which he argued that new computer technologies will make representative democracy obsolete because they will make it possible to have instant plebiscites on every issue.[3] In this way, American voters will directly decide if we should join a trade agreement, send troops to Bosnia, or impeach the president. The Senate and the House of Representatives will be largely unnecessary. This, Grossman said, is participatory democracy just as it was in Athens in the 5th century B.C. Now, I have no objection to borrowing a phrase from an older media environment to try to conceptualize a new development. We do it all the time, but it has its risks and attention must be paid when it is done. To call a train an *iron horse,* as we once did, may be picturesque but it obscures the most significant differences between a train and a horse and buggy. To use the term an *electronic town hall meeting* similarly obscures the difference between an 18th-century face-to-face gathering of citizens and a packaged televised pseudo-event.

As has been done elsewhere in this book, to use the term *distance learning* to refer to students and a teacher sending email messages to each other might have some value, but it obscures the fact that the active reading of a book is the best example of distance learning possible, for reading not only triumphs over the limitations of space and copresence, but of time as well. As for participatory democracy, we would be hard-pressed to find any similarity whatsoever between politics as practiced by 5,000 homogenous, well-educated, slave-holding Athenian men and 250 million Americans doing plebiscites every week, and it is dangerous to allow language to lead us to believe otherwise. Of particular interest, I should think, is the effect technology has had on such essential words as *truth, law, intelligence,* and *fact.* To get at these changes, one has to do some historical study—for example, to learn how writing changed the meeting of *truth* and *law*, or how the printing press altered the meaning of *intelligence.*

I am not saying, by the way, that we ought to resist language change, only that we be aware of how it occurs, and why, and what sorts of attitudes language change promotes.

WHO AND WHAT ACQUIRE POWER DUE TO TECHNOLOGICAL CHANGE?

Here is the final question. It is related to some of the others, but I give it special status because of its importance: "What sort of people and institutions acquire special economic and political power because of technological change?" This question needs to be asked because the transformation of a technology into a medium always results in a realignment of economic and political power. I do not say this as a criticism of anyone, but simply as a fact. A new medium creates new jobs and makes old ones obsolete. A new medium gives prominence to certain kinds of skills and subordinates others. Ronald Reagan, for example, could not have been president were it not for television. This is a man who rarely spoke precisely and never eloquently; yet he was called the Great Communicator. Why? Because he was magic on television. His televised image projected a sense of authenticity, tradition, intimacy, and caring and it did not matter if citizens agreed with what he said, or even understood what he said. Television gives power to some and it deprives others. This is true of every important medium. This fact has always been understood by intelligent entrepreneurs who see opportunities emerging from the creation of new media. That is why media entrepreneurs are the most radical force in a culture. They are interested in maximizing profits of new media and do not give much thought to large-scale cultural effects.

I might add that sometimes media entrepreneurs will lie to the public about cultural effects to keep the public mind calm. For example, we have been told that computer technology is good for the environment because there will be less paper required and therefore fewer trees to cut down; but, of course, the opposite has happened. Computer technology has resulted in our using more paper than ever. To take another example, media entrepreneurs tell the public that, in the long run, computers will increase the number of jobs available, but this is nonsense, and it amazes me that anyone could believe it. The simple fact is that computers do what people are accustomed to doing and they can do it faster and cheaper. Be that as it may, in America, our greatest radicals have been our media entrepreneurs—Morse, Bell, Edison, Sarnoff, Disney—these men created the 20th century, as Bill Gates and others are creating the 21st. I do not know if much can be done to moderate the cultural changes that media entrepreneurs will enforce, but citizens at least ought to know what is happening and keep an attentive eye on such people.

There are many other questions that I could suggest, but here I will stick with these six: What problem is solved by a new technology? Whose problem is it? What new problems are created by solving an old one? What people and institutions might be harmed? What changes in language will result? Who will be given new powers?

As the reader considers each question discussed in this chapter, I hope the impression is not left that they represent the outlook of a particular political ideology. As I see them, or at least intend them to be seen, these questions are not the questions of radicals, liberals, conservatives, or any other politics. The answers one gives may have an ideological cast, but the questions are those of anyone who wishes to begin understanding media, and my hope is that they will be taken as seriously as I take them.

ENDNOTES

1. Babington, Charles, "MD Launches a 'Net Effort; $53 Million Plan Would Plug in Public Schools," *The Washington Post,* 13 June, 1996, Final Edition.

2. Thoreau, Henry David, *Walden, or Life in the Woods,* Boston, Ticknor and Fields, 1854.

3. Grossman, Lawrence K., *The Electronic Republic: Reshaping Democracy in the Information Age,* New York, 1995.

8

FIVE GREAT PROMISES OF E-LEARNING

As the youngest of the contributors to this book, I have no memory of life without some form of a personal computer. Far from inoculating me with a worldview that takes the rapid change of technology in stride, I am perhaps the most aware and astonished by how much has changed, so quickly. When I was in elementary school, I tapped away entering text BASIC commands on a home Atari 800 system. To this day, the most mind-blowing advance in technology I have ever experienced was when I saw my first hard drive (external, of course) attached to a friend's computer. Soon the days of constantly swapping disks would be gone, although I couldn't afford one for myself at the time.

By college, my computer was upgraded to an Atari 1040ST with the GEM graphical user interface. By the time I left for graduate school four years later, a black-and-white Toshiba laptop running Windows 3.5 was my computer of choice, although I preferred DOS commands all the same. I had heard of email in college, but not the Web, and only slightly grasped the power of the Internet through a Gopher network demonstration given to me by a friend in the university's IT shop.

Fast forward to today, and whereas six years ago not a single one of my undergraduate courses used any form of electronic support beyond word processing, today every single course I take as a doctoral student now has a Web site, assigned Web readings, ongoing Web-based discussion postings, and the like. At institutions running my company Blackboard's software alone, more than 3.5 million faculty and students generate more than 300 million page views a month, with students spending an average 60 minutes in the system each session. Although the largest, we are but one of several major providers of technology for e-learning.

In short, I have learned firsthand the power of change in technology. With decades of change ahead, there is no doubt in my mind that in its fifth year of mainstream adoption, the sophistication of e-learning in higher education today is only a fraction of what it should and will be in the near future. What is next? With the humility of someone who knows the speed and rapidity of change firsthand, I briefly outline five predictions for your consideration as the final chapter of the book: convergence of modalities, an explosion of sophistication in systems and tools, new insights through data mining, the emergence of the lifelong learner profile, and ubiquitous online academic communities.

PREDICTION 1: CONVERGENCE OF MODALITIES

It is difficult to engage in a discussion of e-learning today without someone asking the question, "What do you mean by e-learning?" Segmentations exist between e-learning that supplements a traditional classroom experience and e-learning that involves complete distance learning in which students never meet face to face: e-learning that is synchronous involving same-time "live" interactions by students online regardless of geography, vs. asynchronous e-learning where students interact with the online course environment at a time of their own choosing; instructor-led e-learning where a faculty member still serves the role of guide and facilitator, as opposed to self-paced e-learning, where the environment is prebuilt and experienced by the student through navigation that takes cues from how the learner performs as he or she goes along; and e-learning that is completely online, vs. e-learning that draws on CD-ROMs and other devices for content. And the list goes on.

It is curious but not surprising that entire educational programs and companies have placed flags in the ground on behalf of just one modality. Their champions tend to argue the merits of one approach at the expense of another. As a result, perhaps 90 percent of e-learning builds on only one or two of the myriad modalities available. My first prediction, therefore, is that 10 years from now modalities will converge, and the basis of description for an e-learning program will be its subject, pedagogy, and target learner, with modalities that best suit all three.

For example, Duke University's oft-cited online global executive MBA program mixes a largely online course delivery experience with once-a-year visits to the Duke campus for intensive face-to-face courses. The result is much of the flexibility that an online program offers for global executives, with an on-campus experience that can ground the participants further. University of Phoenix Online, one of the most successful online degree programs, is known for the face-to-face study groups its students organize in their local areas above and beyond the online course environment. In November 2001, Phoenix announced FlexNet, a degree program that purposefully blends online and classroom-based instruction for convenience and speed. Across the country in Washington, DC, for-profit Strayer University began its successful online university as a "makeup" offering for students who missed a course or two during the semester and needed a way to stay on track.

The University Alliance, a joint venture formed by several Ivy League institutions to offer online distance-learning courses to their alumni, expects to begin every course with a lecture at homecoming and end every course with a session at alumni weekend; the Web supports the course in between. Similarly, more and more courses are designed with a mixture of asynchronous and synchronous experiences. Students largely move through the course at their own pace, reading assignments, taking quizzes and the like, and from time to time they meet in a virtual chat environment to ask questions and "hear" from a speaker (the chat sessions may then be archived for self-paced access later).

Indeed, over time, what we describe today as an e-learning/asynchronous/self-paced course will simply become a course again, with modality selected and described based on the preference of the learner. Breezing through a course catalog, students will expect courses that meet twice a week, once a month, as a whole, in smaller groups, and so on, without thinking of them as different per se. (Chapter 5, "Quality, Cost, and Access: The Case for Redesign," articulates better than I the value and potential of this type of creative redesign.)

PREDICTION 2: NEW AND MORE SOPHISTICATED ACADEMIC TECHNOLOGIES

Not too long ago, the term *academic computing* or *instructional technologies* would have elicited visions of HyperCard, the popular technology from Apple Computer that has long been used to develop instructional supplements. CD-ROMs that provide question drills might have come to mind a close second. In the last five years, with the growth of the Internet, the breadth and choice of instructional technologies has gained incredible steam. Today's faculty and specialists can choose from virtual classroom tools, simulation tools, discussion board tools, collaboration tools, content management and authoring tools, streaming media tools, assessment tools, and so on.

Although the number of options has increased, we are still only at the beginning. For the most part, the tools that exist are designed to support the generic activities of teaching with technology (i.e., quizzing). Among technologies missing are tools that support the varied subjects and teaching styles that comprise the full constellation of in-

struction that exists (i.e., specialized mathematical nota-
tion tools that allow a faculty member to walk students
through complicated math formulas over the Web). In addition to being fairly generic, today's technologies have difficulty supporting the range of novice to sophisticated users,
all within a common interface.

Accentuating the current limitations, many of the tools
sold in the marketplace today are still early in their development and have been known to break down just when
they are needed the most. Too often they crash, frustrating
students and faculty alike. Sold independently of one another, they do not integrate together so that a quizzing
product from one company can be "launched" by a virtual
chat tool from another, the way that a user can click on an
attachment in an email and know that the computer will
load the appropriate software application needed to open
the file. Given that the market is still early in its development, many of the tool providers are young companies that
from time to time become financially insolvent and close,
leaving users in a bind.

As gloomy as this description of the current state of
the academic technology market reads, my second prediction is that within 10 years the state of affairs will look
very different. A broad range of learning applications will
be available for faculty and institutions to assemble as
their needs require. The technologies will support common standards for greater interoperability, and they will

improve through the same cycle of maturity and usability that Windows did, moving from Windows 1.0 to Windows XP, including plenty of ups and downs along the way. Already, course management systems are beginning to serve much the same role as an operating system does on a personal computer. The core system for creating and managing online course environments, institutions are integrating third-party tools into course management systems so that faculty and students experience all of the learning applications they need in one user interface. Services, such as security, tracking, and session management, are provided by the course management system to third-party tools as seamlessly as to the tools that are native to the system. For example, a course management system may come with a discussion board technology as part of the core system. As the choices of various tools increase, a faculty member might wish to switch out the bundled discussion board with one that fits a specific need, knowing that the third-party tool will run as seamlessly within the environment as the original discussion board.

As e-learning adoption grows, the demand by academic institutions for technologies will expand, enabling a viable business climate for companies to grow profitably and invest in future technologies. Much as in the desktop computing world, a few large companies will provide a broad array of technologies, and boutique companies that specialize in a specific product area will meet niche needs in the disciplines. Most important, university-developed applications will become a big piece of the puzzle, and institutions will share tools as shareware or for-profit products. Today's breadth of products will look anemic in comparison and faculty will wonder how they made do.

A powerful example is Pennsylvania State University's School of Information Science and Technology (IST). A full school of the University, IST provides undergraduate and graduate degrees both at the main State College campus and at several branch campuses of the Penn State system. Designed around a structured curriculum, and faced with the challenge that students and faculty move between branch locations, the technology staff developed a series of content management applications. These tools allow IST to maintain a core curriculum of teaching materials and exercises online, with the confidence that a professor three years later could reference a case from the student's freshman year and know that every student would understand the reference and draw a similar conclusion from the comment—regardless of whether the student was a freshman at the Altoona campus or at Allegheny. To make this possible with faculty who naturally want to make their own adjustments to the course, various new tools were developed for publishing, updating, and modifying the content. In addition, tracking systems were developed to ensure that all students completed the core curriculum of each course before moving on. Although much of the success has to do with curriculum design and policies, the technologies developed are critical and can be of great value to other institutions.

PREDICTION 3: DATA MINING

As a broad range of new learning technologies becomes deployed, new forms of data follow closely behind. Already, colleges and universities have modernized many of their administrative systems. As a result, they have access to a variety of demographic and performance data, in relational databases, as never before. For example, an institution can tie course registration data to the student degree requirements and notify the student when a required course is close to being filled. Most universities have not developed their policies and created the "business logic" necessary for the data to be used in such ways, but the potential is there.

As you might imagine, however, administrative data is only part of the overall equation. Although a student record system may know that I passed a course with a B+ in a general math course, it has no idea what my performance was on the specific assessments delivered over the semester that formed the grade. This data would naturally be useful for mapping decisions about future courses that specialize in various topics covered in the course, some of which I may have aced and others of which I may have only barely commanded.

The growth of academic support systems, such as course management systems, is capturing a whole new category of data. Whereas the discussions and activities that occur in a physical classroom leave few artifacts, those that are supported by a Web environment are fully tracked and leave well-structured data for as long as the course is archived. Information on everything from course attendance to the frequency of postings in course Web sites, to topic-by-topic student performance, and more is sitting in campus databases. Perhaps the institution wants to compare the frequency of my Web postings in two different courses as an error check on the degree to which a faculty member elicits class participation. Soon the institution can. Perhaps a faculty member wants to review my performance in an earlier course, to gain insight into why I am struggling in a certain advanced topic? Soon he or she can.

The practice of data mining has traditionally been applied in the corporate world (e.g., the mining of retail sales data by a clothing chain to gain better insight into the success of certain fashions, the difference in consumer demand by geography, etc.). In an academic setting, back-office data is rarely analyzed for insight; instead reports focus on variance from expected targets in areas such as enrollment yield, financial aid applications, and course evaluation completions. As for the data generated by e-learning, even less analysis is done given the newness of the systems. The generic technology for data mining has improved greatly, but sorting through terabytes of information searching for correlations between unrelated information isn't easy. Lack of integration between administrative and academic system data, and the unfamiliarity of administrators with the data collected to even imagine what can be done, are significant obstacles.

As a result, my third prediction is that within 20 years—this one will take longer—data mining will be an effective and common practice at colleges and universities. The new information being generated through e-learning environments will merge with traditional administrative data, providing a new degree of insight with which administrators can make decisions. Consider a process such as reaccredidation of an institution's academic programs and the self-study that goes along with it. Most of the measures reported today as a proxy for quality education are input based: books in the library, expenditures per student, faculty salaries, and so on. Soon, the reaccredidation team will arrive to review the quality of education by qualitatively reviewing archived e-learning environments and by reviewing longitudinal and latitudinal data that analyze faculty over time, students over time, and more.

PREDICTION 4: THE LEARNER PROFILE

Perhaps the most important frontier of data that will grow and take form is in the area of the learner profile. Although most elementary and secondary students in America live in fear of their "permanent record," no such file really exists. Despite the importance of human capital in our society, no single profile aggregates formal and informal education and training records to provide employers with a comprehensive view of someone's ability. Résumés are rarely insightful, and they may contain inaccuracies or half-truths. Even more important, they are useless in helping a manager make assignment and training decisions based on a skill as specific as knowing how to service one type of engine but not another. A need exists to provide one source for verifying both broad credentials and specific skills—what Levine described as a "learning passport" in Chapter 2, "Higher Education: A Revolution Externally, Evolution Internally."

Consider the analogy of what Equifax and other credit bureaus have done in the financial world. Once upon a time, credit information about consumers was stored by the various businesses with which a credit arrangement was formed. Each time a consumer sought to establish credit, the new merchant had no simple way of verifying credit history and making a decision. As a result, the consumer was forced to store and update countless paper records, and the vendor lived in fear of the accuracy and completeness of the information being provided. Over time, credit bureaus evolved to centralize the data, verify it, and make it available through a secure, permission-based process.

Given the vital importance of a comprehensive and accurate learner profile, my fourth prediction is that within 20 years the emergence of an Equifax for human capital will occur. The learner profile will redefine and give meaning to the permanent record, including letters of reference, example work products, training certificates, formal degrees, and more. Each of these high-level accomplishments will have specific skill competencies mapped to them, enabling a granular view of a person's capabilities to inform admissions, hiring, and training decisions.

The challenges of making this a reality are immense, but from a business standpoint, the financial rewards are equally large. Imagine a revenue model of per-degree credential-verification fees associated with the hundreds of millions of hiring and admissions decisions made each year! Indeed, universities could flip the current expense approach of verifying credentials at no fee into a revenue stream.

However, the challenge of aggregating and verifying the data is reminiscent of the "chicken and the egg" dilemma. People will not establish profiles unless there is a universe of employers that require or prefer them, and organizations will not use them unless there are enough profiles to make a meaningful difference. Equally daunting is the difficulty of technically aggregating data from tens of thousands of education and training entities that store them, as well as defining a taxonomy of skills to which various certifications and degrees can be mapped (i.e., within the accounting profession, a classification of various auditing competencies such as valuation or revenue recognition). No doubt, the debate over privacy and information rights that often surrounds the credit bureaus would be even more significant for profiles of learner data.

Nevertheless, in a knowledge economy, human capital is critical. Over time, many of the infrastructure services that enable our systems of financial capital will need to be adapted in the same way.

PREDICTION 5: UBIQUITOUS WEB COMMUNITIES AND SERVICES

My final prediction of a major change that e-learning will bring to higher education is the one that is closest to my heart. My fifth prediction is that universities will maintain ubiquitous Web environments that are personalized, are cohesive, are as critical to the campus community as the quad of old, and can be the spark for a renewed focus on social networks in the education process.

In my experience, the place where e-learning can be most effectively leveraged to improve education is in the support of community in the traditional campus model—social structures, not physical, technological, or administrative structures. Indeed, when partisans of total virtual campuses or total brick-and-mortar campuses sit down and plead their case, they often describe a common underlying strength to both approaches—community (or social capital).

Broadly defined as the trust and norms that social networks produce, social capital has long been a theoretical construct with promising implications for the delivery of education. In short, social capital describes the values, norms, trust, and sense of reciprocity created by closed social networks in communities and organizations. Much as physical, human, and financial capital have come to describe the tangible and intangible resources that drive outputs in organizations, social capital describes the value created in highly networked communities. For example, two organizations with smart people and cash can achieve very different business results based on the team environment and shared norms of the group.

Originally developed by sociologist James Coleman, social capital theory has been most recently (and prominently) applied by Harvard professor Robert Putnam in a study of identical governmental structures in Italy.[1] In his research, Putnam found that quantities of social capital—operationalized through a variety of measures of community engagement—strongly correlated with different levels of effectiveness in otherwise identical public institutions. He then went further and traced the histories of northern and southern Italy, and tied many of his social capital findings with the evolution of social structures in the regions.

When you consider the incredible similarities between how education is carried out at various campuses in America—whether public, private, two-year, or four-year—Putnam's findings raise compelling questions about what factors really make education organizations effective. Like regional governments in Italy, schools and universities in America operate with similar structures in dramatically different cultural contexts, and not all institutions produce high-achieving students at the same rate. In addition, the education process is powerfully influenced by social capital—norms and trust—generated by, and for, families and communities.

Since the early 1980s, social capital theory has been relied on by a small group of researchers in studies ranging from the differences between private and public school achievement, to family characteristics and their influence on academic achievement, to strategies for supporting at-risk students. Looking through the lens of social capital, the most promising targets for e-learning initiatives on campus are those that strengthen the bonds established between faculty members and students, among students themselves, and among faculty—the whole network of connections.

The University of California at Berkeley's respected and long-time investigator of student attitudes and behavior, Sandy Astin, has noted that the "growth in interpersonal skills have to do with student–student interactions: hours per week spent visiting with friends, giving presentations in class, socializing with students from racial or ethnic groups, participating in a college internship program, participating in intramural sports, discussing racial or ethnic issues, and hours per week spent partying."[2]

His examples are drawn largely from outside the classroom. Beyond the four hours of instruction each week per course, it is critical that the environment across the campus sparks interactions that foster a sense of reciprocity and trust. At some of the finest small liberal arts colleges, the claim of a "better education" is not simply a factor of the college's size, but rather the fact that they are more integrated—more connected to the larger purposes of teaching and learning. That goes for the Ivy League schools as well.

As I visit campuses, I am struck by the degree to which many of the most popular uses of e-learning technologies are those that reinforce the notion of an academic community. Students, outside of their regular class sessions, can engage in an ongoing dialogue on the subject of the course through the Web. Students in class for an hour on Monday morning no longer need to wait until Wednesday to ask the questions that came to mind after they left that class. Every afternoon, or possibly in the evening, students can email their professor and get answers that same day or the next, thereby saving class time later. Faculty members are free to dispense with tedious administrative details before even coming to class, allowing for a full hour of lecturing and exchanges with students, instead of 45 or 50 minutes after papers are handed out and the like. Toward these ends, faculties are increasingly embracing the Internet with enthusiasm.

In his landmark work, *Campus Life—In Search of Community,* the late Ernest Boyer noted that a college or university is "an educationally purposeful community, a place where faculty and students share academic goals and work together to strengthen teaching and learning on campus. . . . It is in the classroom where community begins, but learning also reaches out to departments, to residential halls, to the campus commons."[3] In short, Boyer saw colleges and universities as places where campus life is connected at all levels for all participants—faculty and students—who are thereby empowered.

For these reasons, it is no surprise that most widespread Internet usage on campus has taken off in a grass-roots form in activities that augment traditional campus-based education. Surely this is an area where the Internet has a powerful role to play. Indeed, the potential for the first time is a 24/7 connection among all campus members—students, faculty, and administrators. The brick-and-mortar classroom, which has long been the organizing vehicle of the course, is only available two or three days a week when instruction is being delivered. All of the academic-related activities that Boyer cited are poorly integrated given the limitations of the classroom. Move into the Web world, however, and an ever-present course Web site can take over as the hub in a wheel of curricular and extracurricular activities with infinitely better availability and convenience.

These then are my five predictions. Take them with a grain of salt from a person who still considers the advent of hard drives to be the most amazing technological breakthrough of the PC era.

ENDNOTES

1. Coleman, James S. *"Social Capital in the Creation of Human Capital,"* *American Journal of Sociology,* (supplement) 94 (1998): S95-S120.

2. Astin, Alexander W., *What Matters in College: Four Critical Years Revisited,* Jossey-Bass, Incorporated Publishers, 1993.

3. Boyer, Ernest, *"Campus Life—In Search of Community,"* Princeton Press, April 1, 1990.

INDEX

8 reasons why you should read the Financial Times for 4 weeks RISK-FREE!

To help you stay current with significant
developments in the world economy ...
and to assist you to make informed business
decisions — the Financial Times brings you:

① Fast, meaningful overviews of international affairs ... plus daily
briefings on major world news.

② Perceptive coverage of economic, business, financial and political
developments with special focus on emerging markets.

③ More international business news than any other publication.

④ Sophisticated financial analysis and commentary on world market
activity plus stock quotes from over 30 countries.

⑤ Reports on international companies and a section on global investing.

⑥ Specialized pages on management, marketing, advertising and
technological innovations from all parts of the world.

⑦ Highly valued single-topic special reports (over 200 annually)
on countries, industries, investment opportunities, technology and more.

⑧ The Saturday Weekend FT section — a globetrotter's guide to
leisure-time activities around the world: the arts, fine dining, travel,
sports and more.

FT FINANCIAL TIMES
World business newspaper

The *Financial Times* delivers a world of business news.

Use the Risk-Free Trial Voucher below!

To stay ahead in today's business world you need to be well-informed on a daily basis. And not just on the national level. You need a news source that closely monitors the entire world of business, and then delivers it in a concise, quick-read format.

With the *Financial Times* you get the major stories from every region of the world. Reports found nowhere else. You get business, management, politics, economics, technology and more.

Now you can try the *Financial Times* for 4 weeks, absolutely risk free. And better yet, if you wish to continue receiving the *Financial Times* you'll get great savings off the regular subscription rate. Just use the voucher below.

Where to find tomorrow's best business and technology ideas. TODAY.

- Ideas for defining tomorrow's competitive strategies — and executing them.

- Ideas that reflect a profound understanding of today's global business realities.

- Ideas that will help you achieve unprecedented customer and enterprise value.

- Ideas that illuminate the powerful new connections between business and technology.

ONE PUBLISHER.

Financial Times Prentice Hall.

WORLD BUSINESS PUBLISHER

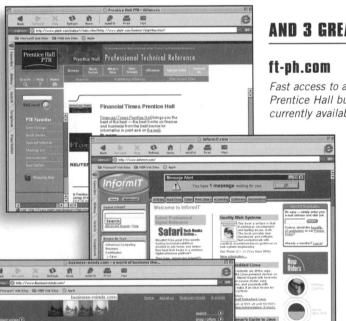

AND 3 GREAT WEB SITES:

ft-ph.com

Fast access to all Financial Times Prentice Hall business books currently available.

InformIt.com

Your link to today's top business and technology experts: new content, practical solutions, and the world's best online training.

Business-minds.com

Where the thought leaders of the business world gather to share key ideas, techniques, resources — and inspiration.

DATE DUE

OC 13 '02			

DEMCO 38-296